كتاب العلم

The Book Of Knowledge

Volume One

Shaykh Muhammad Ibn Saalih al-'Uthaymeen
- may Allaah have mercy upon him .

Translated by
Abu 'Abdullaah Mohammed Akhtar Chaudhry

The Book of Knowledge - Volume One
First Edition, Dhul-Qi'dah 1424 / January 2004 - Invitation To Islaam
Second Edition, Ramadhaan 1431 / September 2010

Copyright © Fatwa-Online Publishing 2001
www.fatwa-online.com | www.efatwa.com

فَمَن كَانَ يَرْجُواْ لِقَآءَ رَبِّهِۦ فَلْيَعْمَلْ عَمَلًا صَٰلِحًا وَلَا يُشْرِكْ بِعِبَادَةِ رَبِّهِۦٓ أَحَدًۢا

*"So whoever hopes for the Meeting with his Lord, let him work righteousness
and associate none as a partner in the worship of his Lord."*
The Noble *Qur.aan* - Soorah al-Kahf, Aayah 110

A CIP catalogue record for this book is available from the British Library
ISBN 9781907589010

Every effort has been made to fulfil requirements with regard
to reproducing copyright material. The Publisher will be
glad to rectify any omissions at the earliest opportunity.

Compilation - Fahd ibn Naasir ibn Ibraaheem as-Sulaymaan

Translation, Cover Design, - Abu 'Abdullaah Mohammed Akhtar Chaudhry
Typesetting and Layout

Published by - Fatwa-Online Publishing
al-Madeenah an-Nabawiyyah
Saudi Arabia
eMail: publishing@fatwa-online.com

Distributed by - Darussalam International
146 Park Road
London NW8 7RG
United Kingdom
Tel: +44.20.8539.4885
Fax: +44.20.8539.4889
eMail: info@darussalam.com

Translator's Dedication

This humble effort is dedicated to the memory of the *Imaam*, the *Zaahid*, the *Faqeeh*, the *'Allaamah*, *Shaykh* Muhammad ibn Saalih al-'Uthaymeen (*rahima-hullaah*):

I first met the *Shaykh* in *Ramadhaan* 1414 *Hijree* / February 1994, when a group of British and American students were invited to sit with him after the *'Asr* prayer in a private room within *al-Masjid al-Haraam*, *Makkah*.

I was fortunate to have met the *Shaykh* a number of times since. My last meeting with the *Shaykh* was when I accompanied him to his hotel after his daily lecture proceeding the *Fajr* prayer in *al-Masjid al-Haraam* on 28 *Ramadhaan* 1420 *Hijree* / 27 December 1999.

The demise in the health of the *Shaykh* hurt us all much, and the news of his death caused many to tremble, particularly when we reflect upon the statement of the *Shaykh*s in Jordan who stated that the calamity in losing *Shaykh* Ibn 'Uthaymeen was actually greater than that of the loss of both *Imaam* Ibn Baaz and *Imaam* al-Albaanee, both of whom passed away in 1999. The reason being that:

"...when the first one died, we said two of them still remain, and when the second one died we said, the third one still remains, and then when the last of them has (now) died, then here we say, with sadness that fills the hearts and tears that fill the eyes, 'who has remained?'..."

We pray to Allaah that he grants those who remain from the *Imaam*s of *Ahlus-Sunnah* and its *Shuyookh* much success in clarifying the way that was traversed by those that have passed away, aameen.

From Abul-Ahwas from 'Abdullaah (ibn Mas'ood):

"Let not any one of you blindly follow in his religion any person such that if he believes, you believe and if he disbelieves you disbelieve. But if you (wish to be) followers (of any one), then (follow) those who have passed away, for verily, the living one is not secure from tribulation."

And also from Masrooq from 'Abdullaah (ibn Mas'ood):

"Do not blindly follow men with regard to your religion, but if you refuse, then by the dead, not the living." (al-Laalikaa.ee 1/93).

بسم الله الرحمن الرحيم

Contents

Translator's Note to First Edition

Indeed all praise is due to Allaah alone, who has allowed this book - **"The Book of Knowledge" - Volume One**, to be made available in the English language. We pray to Him to grant favour upon this effort and to make it of benefit to both Muslims and non-Muslims. May Allaah guide us all to the 'right path', the path of the Prophet, Muhammad (*sal-Allaahu 'alayhi wa sallam*), and His Companions (*radhi-yAllaahu 'anhum*).

Firstly, whoever finds any mistake in the following work; either in the translation or typesetting, then please write to me (at my email address), indicating the mistake and its location, along with the correct translation.

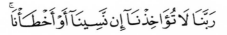

"Our Lord! Punish us not if we forget or fall into error..."[1]

---

1 The Noble *Qur.aan* - *Soorah al-Baqarah, Aayah* 286.

I thank all those who will point out any mistakes and correct the translation with the intention of seeking Allaah's Pleasure. Indeed, Allaah is Surety over what I say.

Additionally, I wish to thank all those involved in this work; from the editors to the proof-readers, and in particular Umm Asmaa and my wife Umm 'Abdullaah.

May Allaah (*Subhaanahu wa Ta'aala*) reward us and all of them with *al-Firdaws - aameen*.

May Allaah humble us all to make this effort pure; seeking His Face alone - certainly to Him is our return.

"Our Lord accept from us, certainly you are the All-Hearing and All-Knowing."[2]

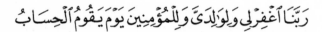

"Our Lord forgive me and my parents, and the believers on the Day when the reckoning will be established."[3]

---

2 The Noble *Qur.aan - Soorah al-Baqarah, Aayah* 127.

3 The Noble *Qur.aan - Soorah Ibraaheem, Aayah* 41.

بِعَوْنِ اللهِ تَعَالَى،

وَ الْحَمْدُ لله الَّذي بِنِعْمَتِه تَتِمُّ الصَّالِحَات

With the assistance of Allaah the Most High, and
all Praise be to Allaah by whose favour good
works are accomplished.[4]

Abu 'Abdullaah Mohammed Akhtar Chaudhry
Faculty of *Sharee'ah*
Islaamic University of Madeenah
al-Madeenah an-Nabawiyyah, Saudi Arabia
al-Jumu'ah 9 *Sha'baan*, 1422 *Hijree* | Friday 26 October, 2001

eMail: abuabdullaah@fatwa-online.com

---

4 Ibn as-Sunnee in *"A'maal al-Yawm wal-Laylah"* and al-Haakim - he declared it
saheeh, 1/499. al-Albaanee declared it *saheeh* in *'Saheeh al-Jaami'* 4/201.

The Importance of Learning the Arabic Language

Whilst every effort has been made to render this translation from it's original Arabic source to English, one must appreciate the rich nature of the Arabic language and how difficult it can be to accurately capture the <u>true</u> essence of the Arabic text in *any* language. Allaah (*Subhaanahu wa Ta'aala*) says:

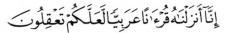

Verily, We have sent it down as an Arabic Qur.aan in order that you may understand.[1]

This book and any other book translated from Arabic should never allow the reader to become complacent and hold back from learning the Arabic language, ever! Rather, it should only serve a <u>temporary</u> purpose in assisting the student of knowledge on his way until he has attained his goal in having learnt the Arabic language.

When I began my Arabic language studies at the Islaamic University of

---

1 The Noble *Qur.aan - Soorah Yoosuf, Aayah* 2.

Madeenah back in 1993, I remember being interviewed by Dr. V. Abdur-Raheem[2] to assess the level of my Arabic knowledge so as to ascertain exactly which class he should enrol me into; It was then that I sought his advice by asking him the question <u>every</u> Arabic language student[3] asks – *"O Shaykh! What is the best way to learn Arabic?"*, whereupon he advised: *"Arabic is not learnt by simply memorising the grammatical rules, rather, Arabic is learnt through necessity..."* – thereby guiding me to restrict my speech to the Arabic language as much as possible despite having <u>just</u> started my studies, *wAllaahul-Musta'aan*!

Poignantly, I recall a popular story our fellow Pakistani students at the

---

2 Author of the popular Duroos al-Lughatil-'Arabiyyah li-Ghayr an-Naatiqeen bihaa - Madeenah Arabic series of books, and at the time, Supervisor of the Institute of Arabic Language at the University. The *Shaykh* is currently the Supervisor of the Translation Department at the King Fahd *Qur.aan* Printing Complex in Madeenah.

3 My personal study notes prepared during my Arabic language studies at the Islaamic University of Madeenah and more study material – are all available for free download at http://www.fatwa-online.com

University narrate about *Shaykh* Ihsaan Ilaahi Zaheer[4]. When the young *Shaykh* arrived at the University as a student he was allocated a room in Building No.2 – which back then accommodated 6 students to a room. Upon discovering all his room mates were fellow Pakistanis he promptly made his way to the Dean of Student Accommodation and filed a complaint stressing that he had come to the University to learn the Arabic language and putting him in a room full of his fellow countrymen was detrimental to his efforts. He politely requested that he be placed in a room full of Arabs, whereupon his request was granted! *Subhaa-nAllaah*! Just listening to his Arabic audio lectures is testament

---

4 Born on 31 May 1945. He studied in Jaami'ah Islaamiyyah Gujranwala and Jaami'ah Salafiyyah Faisalabad. He then started teaching and giving weekly *khutbah*s up until he left for Saudi Arabia. He studied at the Islaamic University of Madeenah and graduated from the Faculty of *Sharee'ah*. During his final year at the Islaamic University of Madeenah, *Shaykh* 'Abdul-'Azeez Ibn Baaz asked him to deliver lectures on the Ahmadiyyah – this is a very rare achievement. His book on the subject was then printed in Madeenah, but the young *Shaykh* wished to include in the book "Graduate of the Islaamic University of Madeenah" – before he had actually graduated! So he asked *Shaykh* Ibn Baaz, who was the Chancellor at the time and he agreed to it. The young *Shaykh* then asked *Shaykh* Ibn Baaz: *"What if I fail my degree?" Shaykh* Ibn Baaz answered: *"I will close the University!"* Upon graduating, he returned to Pakistan and pursued further education and received degree classifications of M.A.s in Arabic, Islaamic Studies, Urdu and Farsi.

He was taught by some of the major scholars of our time – namely: *Shaykh* Abdul Azeez Ibn Baaz, *Shaykh* Muhammad al-Ameen ash-Shanqeetee, *Shaykh* 'Abdul-Muhsin al-'Abbaad, *Shaykh* 'Atiyyah Muhammad Saalim, *Shaykh* Haafidh Muhammad Ghondalwee, *Shaykh* Abul-Barakaat Ahmad and *Shaykh* Muhammad Naasir-ud-Deen al-Albaanee.

He died on 30 March 1987, at the young age of 42; *Shaykh* 'Abdul-'Azeez Ibn Baaz led his funeral prayer in Riyadh, and the secondary prayer in al-Masjid an-Nabawee in Madeenah was attended by thousands. He was buried in the graveyard of al-Baqee' in Madeenah.

to his mastery of the language.

Imaam ash-Shaafi'ee said[5]: *"The language which Allaah favoured was the Arabic language as he revealed his Noble Book in this (Arabic) and he made this the language of the seal of the prophets Muhammad. And that is why we say that it is befitting for everyone who has the ability to learn Arabic – that they learn it, as it is the best language."*

So, just imagine how much you have enjoyed reading a translated book; Now imagine how richer your experience would be if you were to read the original in Arabic!

Regarding the student of knowledge, *Shaykh* al-Albaanee was asked[6]: Is it obligatory upon a student of knowledge to learn and communicate in the Arabic language?

And the *Shaykh* responded: *Learning the Arabic language is an obligatory matter, as has been determined by the scholars, that:*

"If an obligatory act [A] requires you to undertake a secondary act [B] in order to fulfill the obligatory act [A], then that secondary act [B] becomes obligatory."

[That said], it is not possible for a student of knowledge to understand the Qur.aan and the Sunnah except by means of the Arabic language.

As for communicating in Arabic, then it is from the recommended acts, since there is no evidence to suggest its obligation.

---

5 Iqtidaa Siraatil-Mustaqeem - Volume 1, Page 521.

6 *Fataawa* ash-*Shaykh* al-Albaanee fil-Madeenah wal-Imaaraat - Page 35.

Likewise, *Shaykh* Ibn 'Uthaymeen was asked[7]: It is apparent that many students of knowledge steer away from perfecting the rules of the Arabic language (grammar); Considering it's importance – what is your point of view?

And the *Shaykh* responsed: *Yes, understanding the Arabic language is important, whether it be the rules of i'raab or the rules of balaaghah, all of these are important. However, based upon us being Arabs, and all Praise is for Allaah, then it is possible to learn without knowing the rules of the Arabic language. However, from that which is complete (and better) is for a person to learn the rules of the Arabic language. So, I encourage the learning of the Arabic language with all it's rules.*

Likewise, Shaykhul-Islaam Ibn Taymiyyah (*rahima-hullaah*) said[8]: "*It is known that Arabic is Fard 'alal-Kifaayah and the Salaf would discipline their children for making grammatical mistakes. Due to this, we are ordered, whether it be an obligation or a recommendation, to preserve the Arabic (grammatical) rules, and to correct the tongues that have deviated from the correct speech. By doing so, we preserve the methodology of understanding the Qur.aan and the Sunnah. We also preserve the following of the Arabs in their manner of (correct) speech. If people were left with their grammatical mistakes, this would be considered a great deficiency and despicable mistake.*"

Shaykh Ibn 'Uthaymeen was also asked[9]: *Baara-kAllaahu Feekum*, is the fact that the *Qur.aan* was revealed in the Arabic language a justifica-

---

7 Kitaabul-'Ilm - Page 145, Question No.42.

8 Majmoo al-Fataawa - Volume 32, Page 252.

9 Fataawa Noor 'alad-Darb;
   Translated by Abu Abdul-Waahid Nadir Ahmad.

tion or an excuse for non-Arabs (for not acting upon it) due to it not being revealed in their language?

The *Shaykh* responded: *No, non-Arabs do not have an excuse or a justification in that the Qur.aan is not in their language; Rather it is upon them to learn the language of the Qur.aan, because if understanding the Book of Allaah or the Sunnah of the Messenger of Allaah (sal-Allaahu 'alayhi wa sallam) is dependant upon learning the Arabic language, then learning Arabic becomes waajib. This is because every action that has to be carried out, in order to be able to perform an obligation, acquires the ruling of being obligatory [or - All actions which if not performed first, an obligatory act cannot be performed, acquire the ruling of being obligatory (even if they are not an obligation within themselves, such as walking to the masjid for Salaatul Jamaa'ah (for men), since one cannot perform jamaa'ah in the masjid unless he walks there, the act of walking in order to get to the masjid becomes waajib upon that individual, and so on...)].*

Allaah (*Subhaanahu wa Ta'aala*) says:

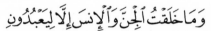

And I created not the jinn and mankind except that they should worship Me (Alone). [10]

In this *aayah*, Allaah (*Subhaanahu wa Ta'aala*) has clearly defined the purpose of our creation – our purpose in this life, and outlined the means which shall assist us upon this path in the Noble *Qur.aan* and the authentic *Sunnah* – both of which originate in the Arabic language.

---

10 The Noble *Qur.aan* - *Soorah adh-Dhaariyaat, Aayah* 56.

Considering this simple, yet essential fact, should provide us sufficient incentive to allocate time from our busy lives to learning Arabic which will subsequently open the doors to acquiring greater knowledge of this blessed religion of ours.

And what greater means to seeking knowledge can there be than to humble ourselves and sit at the feet of the inheritors[11] of the Prophets – the Scholars of *Ahlus-Sunnah* – and take directly fom them!

And as we take from them, we do so in order to worship our Lord upon sound knowledge, as Allaah (*Subhaanahu wa Ta'aala*) says:

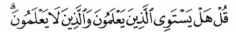

Say: "Are those who know equal to those who know not?"[12]

"So he who worships Allaah upon sound knowledge will find great delight and immense pleasure in his worship, as opposed to he who worships Allaah without sound knowledge."[13] Therefore, as we pursue this noble path, let us recall the words of the Messenger of Allaah (*sal-Allaahu 'alayhi wa sallam*) who said in this regard:

Whoever treads a path in search of knowledge,

---

11 *Saheeh* al-Bukhaaree: Chapter - Knowledge precedes Speech and Action; *Musnad* of *Imaam* Ahmad:
    "...and certainly, the Scholars are the inheritors of the Prophets..."

12 The Noble *Qur.aan* - Soorah az-Zumar, Aayah 9.

13 *Shaykh* Ibn 'Uthaymeen - Fat.h Dhil-Jalaali wal-Ikraam bi-Sharh Buloogh al-Maraam, Book of Purification - Pages 41-42.

Allaah will make easy for him the path to Paradise. [14]

...the <u>ultimate</u> reward!

I close my sincere advice with the case of a sister who strived and struggled to learn the Arabic language, despite the odds; Despite maintaining a 24-hour routine with her husband, both caring for their two terminally ill children with Batten's disease, Zakkee - 12 and Zahraa - 10, she *still* found time to pursue her passion for learning the Arabic language.

Her care shift would finish daily at midnight when I would visit her to teach her for up to an hour, and after I left, she would revise what I had taught her until 2am when she would go to sleep. She would be up again for the *Fajr* prayer and then resume her chare shift at 8am.

My Sister, Umm Zakkee (*rahima-hAllaah*), died of breast cancer in the early hours of Saturday 16th *Ramadhaan* (1st December 2001) at the age of 35 years; Please remember her in your prayers.

May Allaah (*'Azza wa Jall*) permit her notes[15] to benefit all who seek to learn the Arabic language, and may He (*'Azza wa Jall*) cleanse my Sister of her sins and reward her with *al-Firdows al-A'laa*, *aameen*.

---

14 *Saheeh* al-Bukhaaree: Chapter - Knowledge precedes Speech and Action;
   Saheeh Muslim - The Book of Invitations;
   Musnad of *Imaam* Ahmad.

15 "Umm Zakkee's personal study notes to Dr. V. 'Abdur-Raheem's ((Lessons in Arabic Language)) – Book 2; [as taught at the Islaamic University of Madeenah]" – available for free download at http://www.fatwa-online.com

Biography of
Shaykh Muhammad ibn Saalih al-'Uthaymeen
1929-2001

1. His Lineage[1]

He is Abu 'Abdullaah Muhammad ibn Saalih ibn Muhammad ibn al-'Uthaymeen al-Wuhaybee at-Tameemee.

2. His Place of Birth

He was born in the town of 'Unayzah, in the region of Qaseem, on the 27th day of the blessed month of *Ramadhaan* in 1347 *Hijree*.

3. His Early Life

He recited the Noble *Qur.aan* to his maternal grandfather, 'Abdur-Rahmaan ibn Sulaymaan Aal Daamigh (*rahima-hullaah*) and memorised it. Then he directed his attention towards seeking other knowledge and so he learned writing, arithmetic and some other subjects. *Shaykh* 'Abdur-Rahmaan as-Sa'dee (*rahima-hullaah*) used to place two of the students of knowledge that studied with him in charge of teaching the young students. The first of them was *Shaykh* 'Alee as-Saalihee, and the second was *Shaykh* Muhammad ibn 'Abdul-'Azeez al-Mutawwa' (*rahi-*

---

1 Translated by Abu Maryam Ismaa'eel Alercon.

ma-hullaah), under whom he (Ibn 'Uthaymeen) studied the abridged version of *"al-'Aqeedah al-Waasitiyyah"* (of Ibn Taymiyyah), written by *Shaykh* 'Abdur-Rahmaan as-Sa'dee, *"Minhaaj as-Saalikeen fil-Fiqh"*; also by *Shaykh* 'Abdur-Rahmaan, as well as *"al-Aajaromiyyah"* and *"al-Alfi-yyah"*. He also studied the laws of inheritance and *fiqh* under *Shaykh* 'Abdur-Rahmaan ibn 'Alee ibn 'Awdaan.

Under *Shaykh* 'Abdur-Rahmaan ibn Naasir as-Sa'dee (*rahima-hullaah*) - who is considered to be his first teacher as he remained with him for a period of time - he studied the sciences of *tawheed, tafseer, hadeeth, fiqh, usool al-fiqh, faraa.id, mustalah al-hadeeth, nahoo* and *sarf*.

He also studied under the noble *Shaykh*, 'Abdul-'Azeez ibn Baaz, such that he came to be known as his second teacher; with him he began the study of *Saheeh* al-Bukhaaree, some of the treatises of *Shaykh* al-Islaam Ibn Taymiyyah, and some books of *fiqh*.

4. His Precedence in Knowledge and His Work in the Field of *Da'wah*

In the year 1371 *Hijree*, he began to teach in the congregational mosque. When the educational institutes opened in Riyadh, he signed up with them in 1372 *Hijree* and after two years he graduated and was appointed as a teacher at the educational institute (*Ma'had al-'Ilmee*) in 'Unayzah. In the meantime he continued his studies affiliated with the College of *Sharee'ah*, as well as his studies under *Shaykh* 'Abdur-Rahmaan as-Sa'dee (*rahima-hullaah*).

When *Shaykh* 'Abdur-Rahmaan as-Sa'dee passed away, he was given the position of *Imaam* at the main congregational mosque of 'Unayzah, along with the responsibility to teach in the central library of 'Unayzah, in addition to teaching at the educational institute. He later moved on to teaching in the Faculties of *Sharee'ah* and *Usool ad-Deen* in the Qaseem branch of the *Imaam* Muhammad ibn Su'ood Islaamic University. In addition to this, he was appointed a member of the Council of Senior Scholars of the Kingdom of Saudi Arabia.

Shaykh Ibn 'Uthaymeen has played a large and active role in the field of *da'wah* (calling to Allaah) and teaching the Muslims. Thus the people recognised him from the various beneficial classes and impressive sermons he gave on the day of *Jumu'ah* in the Central *Masjid* of 'Unayzah, in Qaseem. They knew him from the lessons he taught in *al-Masjid al-Haraam* during the nights of *i'tikaaf* in the month of *Ramadhaan*, every year. He was also known by the firmly composed *fataawa* he issued to the masses of Muslims from the East and the West; during the joyous occasion of *Hajj*, or in the journals and magazines, on the radio broadcast *"Light upon the Path"* (*Noor 'alad-Darb*), and through the letters he exchanged with many students of knowledge and readers. Furthermore, he was known for the rulings he gave with complete and wholesome responses to the questions that were presented to him everyday.

5. His Books on the Subject of *'Aqeedah*

Shaykh Muhammad ibn Saalih al-'Uthaymeen has a vast number of valuable books from which the people gain benefit; on the subjects of *'aqeedah*, *fiqh* and its principles, admonition, advice and *da'wah*, and a large portion of which are taught by the Ministry of Education of the Kingdom of Saudi Arabia.

We will mention here the books that are related to *'aqeedah*:

1. *Fat.h Rabbil-Barriyyah Bi-Talkhees al-Hamawiyyah*: This is his first book that was ever printed. He completed it on the 8th of *Dhul-Qi'dah* 1380 *Hijree*. It is printed within a collection of essays on *'aqeedah* by Maktabah al-Ma'aarif of Riyadh.

2. *Nubadh fil-'Aqeedah al-Islaamiyyah* (A Brief Article on the Islaamic Creed): In this book the *Shaykh* explains the six pillars of *Eemaan*. It was assigned to the third year of secondary school in the educational institutes, for the subject of *tawheed*. It was printed in the collection mentioned previously of Maktabah al-Ma'aarif of Riyadh.

3. *al-Qawaa'id-ul-Muthlaa fee Sifaatillaah wa Asmaa.ihi al-Husnaa* (Ideal Principles Concerning Allaah's Attributes and His Beautiful Names): It is one of the most magnificent works that *Shaykh* 'Uthaymeen has written. We have provided a checking for it, as well as a commentary on the chains of narration, and it has been printed - all praise is due to Allaah.

4. *Sharh Lum'atul-'Itiqaad al-Haadee ilaa Sabeel ar-Rashaad libni Qudaamah* (An Explanation of "Sufficiency in Creed" - A Guide to the Straight Path - of Ibn Qudaamah): It is this book which was assigned to the first year of the secondary school level of the educational institutes, for the subject of *tawheed*.

5. *'Aqeedah Ahl-us-Sunnah wal-Jamaa'ah* (The Creed of *Ahl-us-Sunnah wal-Jamaa'ah*): He mentions in it a summarised yet comprehensive account of the Creed of *Ahl-us-Sunnah wal-Jamaa'ah*. The Islaamic University of Madeenah printed it.

6. *Sharh al-'Aqeedah al-Waasitiyyah libni Taymiyyah* (An Explanation of the Book, *"al-'Aqeedah al-Waasitiyyah"* of Ibn Taymiyyah): It was assigned to the second year of the secondary school level of the educational institutes, for the subject of *tawheed*. It is printed and in wide circulation.

7. *Tafseer Aayatul-Kursee* (An Explanation of *Aayatul-Kursee*): This tafseer consists of a magnificent topic on the Names and Attributes of

Allaah, discussed by the *Shaykh*. It is printed and in wide circulation. In addition to this, there are all the *fataawa* of the *Shaykh* regarding *'Aqeedah* which have been printed many times over and included in his books on *fataawa*, in magazines, and in journals.

6. His Death

The *Shaykh* (*rahima-hullaah*) passed away on Wednesday, the 15th of *Shawwaal* 1421 *Hijree* (10 January, 2001), when he was 74 years of age. We pray to Allaah that the Muslims benefit from what he has left behind of his knowledge and wisdom, and to grant him due reward and forgiveness for his sins.

Chapter One

Definition of Knowledge,
it's Virtues and the Ruling Regarding Seeking it.

Within this chapter there are three parts:

Part One
The Definition of Knowledge

Part Two
The Virtues of Knowledge

Part Three
The Ruling Regarding Seeking Knowledge

Part One

Definition of Knowledge

Linguistically - (Knowledge is) the opposite of ignorance, which is: To understand something with definitive understanding.

Technically - Some of the people of knowledge have said: (knowledge) *"...is to know (something) and it is the opposite of ignorance,"* while others from amongst them have said: *"Certainly, knowledge is more than to (simply) know."*

What we mean here is knowledge of the *Sharee'ah*, and what is meant by this is: **knowledge which Allaah has revealed to His Messenger from the evidences and the guidance**. Therefore, knowledge which has praise and commendation attached to it is knowledge of the revelation, that being, only knowledge which Allaah has revealed.

The Prophet (*sal-Allaahu 'alayhi wa sallam*) said:

> ***Whoever Allaah wishes good for, He grants him un-***

derstanding of the religion.[1]

The Prophet (*sal-Allaahu 'alayhi wa sallam*) also said:

> ***Certainly, the Prophets have not bequeathed deen-***
> ***aar nor dirham, rather they have bequeathed***
> ***knowledge, so whoever takes it has taken abun-***
> ***dant good fortune.***[2]

From that which is known is that what the Prophets have bequeathed is the knowledge of the *Sharee'ah* of Allaah (*Subhaanahu wa Ta'aala*) and nothing other than it. So, the Prophets (*'alayhimis-salaam*) have not bequeathed for man knowledge of manufacturing and that which is related to it; rather, when the Messenger (*sal-Allaahu 'alayhi wa sallam*) arrived in Madeenah he found the people grafting the date palms. Having seen how tired they had become he said to them something along the lines of, there is no need for this, meaning grafting. Upon hearing this they left the process of grafting, and as a result the date palms deteriorated in their yield. The Prophet (*sal-Allaahu 'alayhi wa sallam*) then said to them:

> ***You have better knowledge (of a technical skill)***
> ***in the affairs of your world.***[3]

Were it that such knowledge was praiseworthy then the Messenger (*sal-*

---

1 *Saheeh* al-Bukhaaree - The Book of Knowledge;
   Saheeh Muslim - The Book of *Zakaah*.

2 Abu Daawood - The Book of Knowledge;
   at-Tirmidhee - The Book of Knowledge.

3 *Saheeh* Muslim - The Book of Virtues.

Allaahu 'alayhi wa sallam) would have been more knowledgeable than the people about it; this is because the one who is most praised and blessed with knowledge and acting upon that knowledge is the Prophet (*sal-Allaahu 'alayhi wa sallam*).

Therefore knowledge of the *Sharee'ah* is that which is praiseworthy, and the one who acts according to it is also praiseworthy.

However, this does not mean that there is no benefit in acquiring other knowledge; rather, at certain times learning it may be obligatory. However there are certain conditions that need to be fulfilled: it must possess a double-edged benefit. If it assists in obedience to Allaah and leads to the success and victory of the Religion of Allaah, and the servants of Allaah are able to benefit from it, then that is good and beneficial knowledge, and learning it may well be obligatory at certain times should it fall under the statement of Allaah (*Subhaanahu wa Ta'aala*):

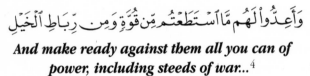

And make ready against them all you can of power, including steeds of war...[4]

It has been mentioned by many from amongst the people of knowledge that seeking knowledge of manufacturing is *fard kifaayah*, and that is for example, because it is imperative that the people have (utensils and) containers to cook with and drink from, and such similar issues with which they can seek benefit. So if there were none who came forward to establish such a process, then the learning of it becomes *fard kifaayah* and this is a controversial issue amongst the people of knowledge. However, I wish to reaffirm that the knowledge which is praiseworthy

---

4 The Noble *Qur.aan* - *Soorah* al-Anfaal, *Aayah* 60.

and commendable is knowledge of the *Sharee'ah*, which is understanding the Book of Allaah and the *Sunnah* of His Messenger *(sal-Allaahu 'alayhi wa sallam)*, and that which is other than this is either a means to something good or a means to something evil. Therefore its ruling is based upon what that particular knowledge is a means to, either good or evil.

Part Two

The Virtues of (Seeking) Knowledge

Allaah (*Subhaanahu wa Ta'aala*) has praised knowledge of the *Sharee'ah* and the people of knowledge, and has encouraged His servants to seek this knowledge, which includes knowledge of the authenticated *Sunnah*.

So seeking knowledge is amongst the most superior and virtuous acts as it is one of the most superior and honourable acts of worship. This is because it is a type of *jihaad* in the Path of Allaah. Certainly, the Religion of Allaah (*Subhaanahu wa Ta'aala*) has been established upon two principles:

Firstly: Knowledge and Evidence;

Secondly: Combat on the battlefield.

These two principles are imperative in establishing the Religion of Allaah, and it is not possible for the Religion of Allaah to be established and prevail without these two principles collectively.

The first of the two principles takes precedence over the second, and because of this the Prophet (*sal-Allaahu 'alayhi wa sallam*) never imposed anything upon a nation until he had conveyed to them the Message of Allaah (*Subhaanahu wa Ta'aala*); therefore knowledge preceded combat.

Allaah (*Subhaanahu wa Ta'aala*) says:

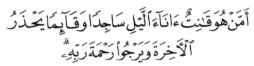

Is one who is obedient to Allaah, prostrating himself or standing during the hours of the night, fearing the Hereafter and hoping for the Mercy of his Lord?[1]

So the issue here is that there must be one who is other than this; is the one who is standing in obedience during the night and day the same as the one who does not do this?

And, is the one who is obedient to Allaah, standing and prostrating himself in prayer during the night, fearing the Hereafter and seeking the Mercy of his Lord, equal to the one who considers himself far above from obedience to Allaah?

The answer: No! He is not equal! So, the one who is obedient to Allaah, seeking the reward from Allaah and fearing the Hereafter, are his actions based upon knowledge or upon ignorance?

The answer: His actions are based upon knowledge and because of this

---

1 The Noble Qur.aan - *Soorah* az-Zumar, *Aayah* 9.

Allaah (*Subhaanahu wa Ta'aala*) says:

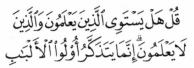

Are those who know equal to those who know not?"
It is only men of understanding who will remem-
ber.[2]

There is no comparison between one who has knowledge and one who does not, just as there is no comparison between the living and the dead; the one who hears and the one who is deaf; and the one who can see and the one who is blind. Knowledge is light with which one is guided, and it removes one from the darkness (of ignorance) to the light (of knowledge, i.e. *Islaam*). With knowledge Allaah (*Subhaanahu wa Ta'aala*) raises the ranks of whom He wishes from His creation:

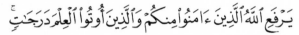

Allaah will exalt in degree those of you who believe,
and those who have been granted knowledge.[3]

Because of this, we find the people of knowledge at the centre of praise; whenever mention is made of them, the people praise them. This is their status in this world. As for the Hereafter, then they will be raised to ranks according to that which they stood for in calling to Allaah and acting according to that which they knew.

Certainly, the true worshipper is he who worships his Lord upon sound

---

2 The Noble *Qur.aan* - *Soorah* az-Zumar, *Aayah* 9.

3 The Noble *Qur.aan* - *Soorah* al-Mujaadilah, *Aayah* 11.

knowledge, and the truth is made clear to him. This is the path of the Prophet (*sal-Allaahu 'alayhi wa sallam*), just as Allaah (*Subhaanahu wa Ta'aala*) says:

قُلْ هَٰذِهِۦ سَبِيلِىٓ أَدْعُوٓاْ إِلَى ٱللَّهِ عَلَىٰ بَصِيرَةٍ أَنَا۠ وَمَنِ ٱتَّبَعَنِى وَسُبْحَٰنَ ٱللَّهِ وَمَآ أَنَا۠ مِنَ ٱلْمُشْرِكِينَ

Say: "This is my way; I invite unto Allaah with sure knowledge, I and whosoever follows me with sure knowledge. And Glorified and Exalted be Allaah. And I am not of the Mushrikeen."[4]

So one who purifies himself and knows this is based upon something from the *Sharee'ah*, is he like the one who purifies himself because he saw his father or his mother doing the same?

Which of the two is more versed in carrying out this act of worship? Is it the one who purifies himself because he knows Allaah (*Subhaanahu wa Ta'aala*) has commanded purification and that this is also the way the Prophet (*sal-Allaahu 'alayhi wa sallam*) purified himself, so he purifies himself in obedience to Allaah (*Subhaanahu wa Ta'aala*) and in accordance with the *Sunnah* of the Messenger of Allaah (*sal-Allaahu 'alayhi wa sallam*)?

Or is it the one who purifies himself because it is something quite ordinary and common to him?

The answer: Without doubt, the first (of the two) is the one who worships Allaah (*Subhaanahu wa Ta'aala*) upon sound knowledge.

---

4 The Noble *Qur.aan* - *Soorah* Yoosuf, *Aayah* 108.

So, is he equal to the other? Even though their actions are one and the same, his actions are based upon sound knowledge, seeking the Mercy of Allaah (*Subhaanahu wa Ta'aala*) and fearing the Hereafter, and he is aware he is following the Messenger of Allaah (*sal-Allaahu 'alayhi wa sallam*).

I pause at this point and ask: should we be conscious when we are making the ablution, that what we are doing is in obedience to the commandment of Allaah (*Subhaanahu wa Ta'aala*)? He (*Subhaanahu wa Ta'aala*) says:

$$\text{يَـٰٓأَيُّهَا ٱلَّذِينَ ءَامَنُوٓاْ إِذَا قُمۡتُمۡ إِلَى ٱلصَّلَوٰةِ فَٱغۡسِلُواْ}$$
$$\text{وُجُوهَكُمۡ وَأَيۡدِيَكُمۡ إِلَى ٱلۡمَرَافِقِ وَٱمۡسَحُواْ بِرُءُوسِكُمۡ}$$
$$\text{وَأَرۡجُلَكُمۡ إِلَى ٱلۡكَعۡبَيۡنِ}$$

O you who believe! When you intend to offer as-Salaah, wash your faces and your hands up to the elbows, rub your heads, and your feet up to ankles. [5]

Should one call to mind this *aayah* when making ablution, and that he is doing ablution in obedience to the command of Allaah?

Should he be conscious that this is the (manner of making) ablution of the Messenger of Allaah (*sal-Allaahu 'alayhi wa sallam*) and that he is doing the ablution in adherence to the *Sunnah* of the Messenger of Allaah (*sal-Allaahu 'alayhi wa sallam*)?

The answer: Yes! In reality, from amongst us there are those who call

---

5 The Noble *Qur.aan* - *Soorah* al-Maa.idah, *Aayah* 6.

this to mind, and because of this, it is obligatory when doing an act of worship that we are doing so in obedience to the command of Allaah thereby actualising sincerity, and that we are adherents of the *Sunnah* of the Messenger of Allaah (*sal-Allaahu 'alayhi wa sallam*).

We know that from the conditions of the ablution is the intention.

However, the purpose of the intention could imply the intention of the action itself, (i.e. ablution) and this is what is looked into in *Fiqh*; it could also imply the intention of the act (i.e. prayer) for which this action (i.e. ablution) is done.

At this stage, it is upon us to be aware of this great act; when we undertake an act of worship we call to mind that we do so in obedience to the command of Allaah, actualising sincerity, and we also call to mind that the Messenger of Allaah (*sal-Allaahu 'alayhi wa sallam*) did such an act and that we are adherents of it, thereby actualising adherence.

This is because from the conditions of the perfection of an action is: **sincerity** (for the Sake of Allaah (*Subhaanahu wa Ta'aala*)) and **adherence** (to the *Sunnah* of the Messenger of Allaah (*sal-Allaahu 'alayhi wa sallam*)).

With these two (conditions), one affirms the testimony that there is none truly worthy of worship except Allaah alone, and that Muhammad (*sal-Allaahu 'alayhi wa sallam*) is the Messenger of Allaah.

We return to what we mentioned at the beginning from the virtues of knowledge; with knowledge one worships his Lord with insight based upon sound proofs, so that one's heart becomes attached to worship thereby becoming illuminated, and he becomes consistent in doing (these) actions, knowing it is worship and not a ritual. Because of this, if he prays accordingly, then he is assured of that which Allaah mentions[6] - that the prayer protects one from every kind of great sin and evil and wicked deed.

From amongst the important virtues of knowledge is that which follows:

1) That it is a legacy of the Prophets: since the Prophets (*sal-Allaahu 'alayhi wa sallam*) did not bequeath *deenaar* nor *dirham*, rather, they bequeathed knowledge, so whoever takes this knowledge, then he has taken abundant good from the legacy of the Prophets (*sal-Allaahu 'alayhi wa sallam*). So we are now in the 15th century (of the *Hijrah* calendar), and if you are from amongst the people of knowledge, then you have received the legacy of Muhammad (*sal-Allaahu 'alayhi wa sallam*), and this is from amongst the greatest of virtues;

2) That it remains forever; whilst property is consumed and eventually ceases to exist. So we have (the example of) Abu Hurayrah (*radhi-yAllaahu 'anhu*) who was from amongst the poorest of the Companions, such that he would become unconscious and collapse from extreme hunger. I ask you in the Name of Allaah, does mention of Abu Hurayrah exist amongst the people in our time or not? Yes, it does exist, and many fold at that! For whoever benefits from his narrations of the Prophet (*sal-Allaahu 'alayhi wa sallam*) there will be reward for Abu Hurayrah. Thus knowledge is preserved, whilst property is consumed and eventually ceases to exist. So it is upon you, O student of knowledge that you

---

6 <u>Translator's Note</u>: The Noble *Qur.aan* - *Soorah* al-'Ankaboot, *Aayah* 45; Allaah (*Subhaanau wa Ta'aala*) says:

إِنَّ ٱلصَّلَوٰةَ تَنْهَىٰ عَنِ ٱلْفَحْشَاءِ وَٱلْمُنكَرِ

Verily, the prayer prevents al-Fahshaa. and al-Munkar.

hold fast to the knowledge you possess, for it is confirmed in the narration of the Prophet (*sal-Allaahu 'alayhi wa sallam*) who said:

> ***When a man dies, his actions come to an end, except for three: recurring charity, or knowledge by which people benefit, or a pious son, who prays for him.***[7]

3) That he who has knowledge does not become tired in protecting it. This is because if Allaah bestows knowledge upon you then its place is in the heart, and there is no need for containers or keys or the like. It is protected in the heart and soul, and in time itself. It is a protector for you, because it protects you from danger, with Allaah's (*Subhaanahu wa Ta'aala*) Permission. So knowledge protects you, whilst the opposite can be said about property; you protect it by placing it in locked up containers, and despite all this you still remain insecure about it;

4) With it one attains the ranks of the martyrs who are upon the truth; and the evidence is Allaah's (*Subhaanahu wa Ta'aala*) saying:

شَهِدَ

ٱللَّهُ أَنَّهُۥ لَآ إِلَٰهَ إِلَّا هُوَ وَٱلۡمَلَٰٓئِكَةُ وَأُوْلُواْ ٱلۡعِلۡمِ قَآئِمَۢا بِٱلۡقِسۡطِ

Allaah testifies that Laa-Ilaaha illa Huwa (none has the right to be truly worshipped but He), and the angels, and those having knowledge; maintaining His creation in Justice.[8]

---

7 *Saheeh* Muslim - The Book of Legacy.

8 The Noble *Qur.aan* - *Soorah* Aal-'Imraan, *Aayah* 18.

So did Allaah say: "Those of wealth?" No! Rather, He said: **"Those having knowledge; maintaining His creation in Justice."** So, proudly, it is enough for you, O student of knowledge, that you seek to be from amongst those who testify in Allaah; that none has the right to be truly worshipped but He (*Laa ilaaha illaa Huwa*), and with the angels, who testify to the oneness of Allaah (*Subhaanahu wa Ta'aala*);

5) That the people of knowledge are one of a group of those in authority, whom Allaah (*Subhaanahu wa Ta'aala*) has commanded to be obeyed, as He (*Subhaanahu wa Ta'aala*) says:

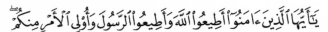

O you who believe! Obey Allaah and obey the Messenger, and those of you who are in authority.[9]

So here 'those in authority' includes those amongst the rulers and governors, and the scholars and the students of knowledge. So the authority of the people of knowledge is in explaining the *Sharee'ah* of Allaah and calling the people to it, whilst the authority of the rulers is in enforcing the *Sharee'ah* of Allaah and enjoining the people in it;

6) That the people of knowledge are upholders of the commandment of Allaah (*Subhaanahu wa Ta'aala*) until the Last Hour. Evidence of this is to be found in the narration of Mu'aawiyah (*radhi-yAllaahu 'anhu*), who said: 'I heard the Prophet (*sal-Allaahu 'alayhi wa sallam*) say:

Whoever Allaah wishes good for, He grants him the understanding of the religion, and I am Qaasim and Allaah is the Provider, and this Ummah will

---

9 The Noble *Qur.aan - Soorah* an-Nisaa., *Aayah* 59.

***always remain upon the command of Allaah and
those who oppose them will be unable to harm
them until the arrival of the command of Allaah
(the Day of Judgement).***[10]

Imaam Ahmad (*rahima-hullaah*) said about this group: *"If they are not
the Ahlul-Hadeeth, then I do not know who they are"*.

And al-Qaadhee 'Iyaadh (*rahima-hullaah*) said: *"Imaam Ahmad meant
the Ahlus-Sunnah and those who believe in the way of the Ahlul-
Hadeeth"*.

7) That the Messenger of Allaah (*sal-Allaahu 'alayhi wa sallam*) did not
encourage anyone to be envious of anyone else over any blessing Allaah
may have bestowed upon them except in two things, which are:

i) Seeking knowledge and acting according to it;
ii) The merchant who has rendered his wealth for the service of *Islaam*.

'Abdullaah ibn Mas'ood (*radhi-yAllaahu 'anhu*) said: 'The Messenger of
Allaah (*sal-Allaahu 'alayhi wa sallam*) said:

> ***Do not be jealous except in two cases. (The first
> is) A person whom Allaah has given wealth and
> he spends it righteously; (The second is) The one
> whom Allaah has given wisdom (the Qur.aan) and***

---

10 *Saheeh* al-Bukhaaree - The Book of Knowledge;
  Saheeh Muslim - The Book of *Zakaah*.

he acts according to it and teaches it to others.[11]

8) That which has been mentioned in a *hadeeth* collected by *Imaam* al-Bukhaaree on the authority of Abu Moosaa al-Ash'aree (*radhi-yAllaahu 'anhu*), that the Messenger of Allaah (*sal-Allaahu 'alayhi wa sallam*) said:

The example of guidance and knowledge with which Allaah has sent me is like abundant rain falling on the earth, some of which was fertile soil that absorbed rain water and brought forth vegetation and grass in abundance. Another portion of it was hard and held the rain water, with which Allaah benefited the people. They utilised it for drinking, watering their animals and for irrigation of the land for cultivation. A portion of it was barren land which could neither hold the water nor bring forth vegetation (so that land gave no benefit). The first is the example of the person who comprehends Allaah's religion, obtains benefit (from the knowledge) that Allaah has revealed through me (the Prophet) and learns and then teaches others. The last example is that of a person who does not care for it and does not take Allaah's guidance revealed through me (he is like that barren land).[12]

---

11 *Saheeh* al-Bukhaaree - The Book of Knowledge;
    Saheeh Muslim - The Book of Prayer.

12 *Saheeh* al-Bukhaaree - The Book of Knowledge;
    Saheeh Muslim - The Book of Virues.

9) That it is a path to Paradise, as indicated in the *hadeeth* of Abu Huray-rah (*radhi-yAllaahu 'anhu*) that the Messenger of Allaah (*sal-Allaahu 'alayhi wa sallam*) said:

Whoever treads a path in search of knowledge, Allaah will make easy for him the path to Paradise.[13]

10) That which occurs in the *hadeeth* of Mu'aawiyah (*radhi-yAllaahu 'anhu*) who said: 'The Messenger of Allaah (*sal-Allaahu 'alayhi wa sallam*) said:

Whoever Allaah wishes good for, He grants him understanding of the religion.[14]

i.e. he makes him fully understand the Religion of Allaah (*Subhaanahu wa Ta'aala*). And understanding of the religion, according to the people of knowledge, does not just mean understanding of the rulings of specific actions, rather, what is meant is that it is: knowledge of *Tawheed* and *Usool ad-Deen* and that which is related to the *Sharee'ah* of Allaah (*Subhaanahu wa Ta'aala*). And if there was no evidence from the *Qur.aan* or the *Sunnah* except this *hadeeth* relating to the virtues of seeking knowledge, then this would have sufficed in encouraging the seeking of knowledge of the *Sharee'ah* and the understanding of it;

---

13 *Saheeh* al-Bukhaaree: Chapter - Knowledge precedes Speech and Action;
   Saheeh Muslim - The Book of Invitations;
   Musnad Imaam Ahmad.

14 *Saheeh* al-Bukhaaree - The Book of Knowledge;
   Saheeh Muslim - The Book of *Zakaah*.

11) That knowledge is light with which the servant seeks guidance, such that he knows how to worship his Lord, and how to interact with His servants, so that his path is built upon knowledge and insight based upon sound proofs;

12) That the scholar is light with which people are guided in their religious and worldly affairs. No doubt many people know the story of the man from the tribe of *Israa.eel* who killed ninety-nine people and then asked about the most knowledgeable person in the land, and he was directed to a pious man. He asked this man if there was any (possibility of) repentance for him. So, the pious man became amazed at the enormity of his actions, and replied, 'No!' So the man killed this pious man and now his count became a complete hundred. Then he approached a scholar and asked him the same question, and was told that there was (a possibility of) repentance for him, and that there was nothing to stand between him and the repentance. He then suggested he travel to such and such a land where the people were upright and virtuous; so he left heading towards it, and he died during the journey. And the story is well known.

So, look at the difference between the scholar and the ignorant!

13) That Allaah (*Subhaanahu wa Ta'aala*) elevates the status of the people of knowledge in this world and the Hereafter. As for the Hereafter, then Allaah will elevate them to ranks according to that which they stood for with respect to their calling to the Path of Allaah (*Subhaanahu wa Ta'aala*) and acting according to what they knew. As for this world, then Allaah will elevate them amongst his servants according to what they stood for. Allaah (*Subhaanahu wa Ta'aala*) says:

يَرْفَعِ ٱللَّهُ ٱلَّذِينَ ءَامَنُوا۟ مِنكُمْ وَٱلَّذِينَ أُوتُوا۟ ٱلْعِلْمَ دَرَجَٰتٍ

Allaah will exalt in degree those of you who believe, and those who have been granted knowledge. [15]

1

---

15 The Noble *Qur.aan* - *Soorah* al-Mujaadilah, *Aayah* 11.

Part Three

The Ruling Regarding Seeking Knowledge

Seeking knowledge of the *Sharee'ah* is *fard kifaayah*. So if someone performs this act, then his act suffices for the rest, and (its performance) then becomes a preferable act (*Sunnah*) for the rest. In certain cases it could also be that the seeking of knowledge is *fard 'ayn* upon some.

Its principle is that when the need to perform an act or to uphold a transaction befalls upon the servant, then it becomes obligatory upon him in this state to know how to engage in the worship of Allaah by this act; and how to uphold this transaction, and any other actions besides these, such as seeking knowledge, are regarded as *fard kifaayah*.

It is befitting for the student of knowledge to be conscious that he is upholding the collective obligation whilst seeking knowledge such that he gains the reward for performing this obligation as well as gaining knowledge.

There is no doubt that seeking knowledge is amongst the most virtuous acts, moreover, it is from *jihaad* in the Path of Allaah, especially in this day and age of ours; where innovations have emerged in the Islaamic society and have increased and become widespread; and the emergence of extreme ignorance from those who aspire to issue *fataawa* without sound knowledge; and the emergence of disputing between many people. So these three issues illustrate the importance upon the youth to seek knowledge:

Firstly, the emergence of innovation and its evil effects;

Secondly, people aspiring to issue *fataawa* without sound knowledge;

Thirdly, the many disputes taking place in religious matters, such that when a matter is clear for the people of knowledge, you find those who lack sound knowledge coming forward and disputing about it.

So, because of this, we are in need of people of knowledge who are firm, upright and possess an abundance of knowledge and understanding of the Religion of Allaah, and have wisdom in advising the servants of Allaah.

Many people nowadays are acquiring theoretical knowledge in religious matters, whilst no importance is attached to reforming and improving neither the people nor their education. And if they issue *fataawa* regarding this and that, then this becomes a means to great evil whereby no-one knows its true extent except Allaah (*Subhaanahu wa Ta'aala*).

Chapter Two

Etiquettes of a Student of Knowledge and
the Means Which Assist in Acquiring Knowledge.

Within this chapter there are two parts:

Part One
Etiquettes of a Student of Knowledge

Part Two
Means Which Assist in Acquiring Knowledge

Part One

Etiquettes of a Student of Knowledge

2

It is imperative for a student of knowledge to have certain etiquettes. Here I shall mention a few:

1. Sincerity of Intention for the Sake of Allaah Alone

Such that one's intention, by seeking knowledge is purely for the Face[1] of Allaah (*Subhaanahu wa Ta'aala*), and success in the Hereafter. This is because Allaah (*Subhaanahu wa Ta'aala*) has encouraged the seeking of knowledge, since He has said:

فَٱعۡلَمۡ أَنَّهُۥ لَآ إِلَٰهَ إِلَّا ٱللَّهُ وَٱسۡتَغۡفِرۡ لِذَنۢبِكَ

So know that Laa ilaaha ill-Allaah (none has the right to be truly worshipped except Allaah, alone), and ask forgiveness for your sin. [2]

And praise for the scholars in the *Qur.aan* is well-known. So if Allaah has

---

1 The Noble *Qur.aan* - *Soorah* ar-Rahmaan, *Aayah* 27.

2 The Noble *Qur.aan* - *Soorah* Muhammad, *Aayah* 19.

praised something or ordered it, then it becomes (an act of) worship.

Therefore, it is obligatory to have sincerity of intention for the Sake of Allaah (*Subhaanahu wa Ta'aala*) alone; that one intends to seek knowledge for the Face of Allaah (*Subhaanahu wa Ta'aala*). And if one were to intend seeking knowledge so that he can attain a certification with which he is able to progress to a higher level, then Abu Hurayrah narrates that the Messenger of Allaah (*sal-Allaahu 'alayhi wa sallam*) said:

> *Whoever acquires knowledge of things by which Allaah's good pleasure is sought, but acquires it only to get some worldly advantage, he will not experience the odour of Paradise (i.e. its beautiful fragrance) on the Day of Judgement.*[3]

This is extremely threatening!

However, if the student of knowledge were to say: 'I wish to attain certification, not because of some worldly affairs, rather because the system dictates the standard of the scholar by his certification.' So we say, if a person's intention is to attain certification so that he can benefit the people by teaching and the like, then this is a sound and true intention and nothing shall harm him.

---

3 *Musnad* of *Imaam* Ahmad - Volume 2, Page 338;
   Abu Daawood - The Book of Knowledge;
   Ibn Maajah - Introduction;
   al-Haakim's *al-Mustadrak* - Volume 1, Page 160;
   Ibn Abee Shaybah's *al-Musannaf* - Volume 8, Page 543;
   al-Haakim said: This is an authentic *hadeeth*, and it's chain of transmitters are reliable.

Indeed, we have mentioned sincerity of intention firstly among the etiquettes of a student of knowledge because sincerity is the foundation. So it is upon the student of knowledge to make the intention when seeking knowledge that he is acting in obedience to the command of Allaah (*Subhaanahu wa Ta'aala*), because Allaah (*Subhaanahu wa Ta'aala*) has commanded the seeking of knowledge, as He has said:

فَٱعۡلَمۡ أَنَّهُۥ لَآ إِلَٰهَ إِلَّا ٱللَّهُ وَٱسۡتَغۡفِرۡ لِذَنۢبِكَ

So know that Laa ilaaha Illa Allaah (none has the right to be truly worshipped except Allaah), and ask forgiveness for your sin. [4]

Therefore, He has commanded the seeking of knowledge. So, if you have sought knowledge, then certainly you are obedient to the command of Allaah (*Subhaanahu wa Ta'aala*).

2. The Removal of Ignorance from Himself and from Others

To make the intention by seeking knowledge, the removal of ignorance from himself and from others, because the natural state of a person is the state of ignorance, and the evidence for this is the saying of Allaah (*Subhaanahu wa Ta'aala*):

وَٱللَّهُ

أَخۡرَجَكُم مِّنۢ بُطُونِ أُمَّهَٰتِكُمۡ لَا تَعۡلَمُونَ شَيۡـًٔا وَجَعَلَ

لَكُمُ ٱلسَّمۡعَ وَٱلۡأَبۡصَٰرَ وَٱلۡأَفۡـِٔدَةَ لَعَلَّكُمۡ تَشۡكُرُونَ

And Allaah has brought you out from the wombs of your mothers while you know nothing. And He

---

4 The Noble *Qur.aan* - *Soorah* Muhammad, *Aayah* 19.

***gave you hearing, sight, and hearts that you might
give thanks.*** [5]

And the reality testifies to this, so make the intention by seeking knowledge, the removal of ignorance from yourself and from others, and with that you acquire the fear of Allaah (*Subhaanahu wa Ta'aala*) as He says:

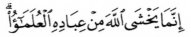

***It is only those who have knowledge among His
slaves that fear Allaah.*** [6]

So make the intention by seeking knowledge, the removal of ignorance from yourself, because your natural state is the state of ignorance. So if you studied and became a scholar, then you have removed ignorance from yourself. Similarly, make the intention by seeking knowledge, the removal of ignorance from the *Ummah*, and this is done through teaching by various means so that you benefit the people with your knowledge.

Is it a condition that benefiting the people with your knowledge means that you hold a study circle in the *masjid*? Or is it possible to benefit the people with your knowledge in any gathering?

<u>The answer</u>: You should benefit the people with your knowledge in any gathering. This is because the Messenger (*sal-Allaahu 'alayhi wa sallam*) said:

---

5 The Noble *Qur.aan - Soorah* an-Nahl, *Aayah* 78.

6 The Noble *Qur.aan - Soorah* Faatir, *Aayah* 28.

52

Narrate from me, even if it is a single verse.[7]

This is because, if you teach someone knowledge and he then teaches another, then you have accrued the reward for teaching two; and if he taught a third, then you have accrued the reward for teaching three and similarly this continues. From this, unfortunately at one extreme, an innovation has begun, whereby if one does an act of worship he says: "Oh Allaah! Render its reward to the Messenger of Allaah".

2

However, since the Messenger (*sal-Allaahu 'alayhi wa sallam*) is the one who taught you this, and he is the one who has guided you to this, his reward is automatically equal to yours.[8]

Imaam Ahmad (*rahima-hullaah*) said: *"Nothing is equivalent to seeking knowledge for one whose intention is correct."*

It was said: *"How is that?"*

He said: *"That he intends with it the removal of ignorance from himself and from others."*

Because the natural state of a person is the state of ignorance if you sought knowledge for the purpose of removing the ignorance from the *Ummah* then you are from amongst the *mujaahideen* in the Path of Allaah; those who propagate the Religion of Allaah.

---

7 *Saheeh* al-Bukhaaree - The Book of Prophets.

8 <u>Translator's Note</u>: There is therefore no need to make this supplication, particularly since it has not been legislated.

3. Advocating the *Sharee'ah*

That he intends by seeking knowledge to advocate the *Sharee'ah*; since it is not possible for the books to advocate the *Sharee'ah*, and none can advocate the *Sharee'ah* except one who knows and understands the *Sharee'ah*. So, if a man from amongst the people of innovation came to a bookshop filled with countless Islaamic books, and began speaking about the promotion of innovation and enforcing it, I do not suppose that even one of those books could appropriately respond to what he is saying. However, if he was to speak about the promotion of innovation and its enforcement in the presence of one from amongst the people of knowledge, then he will be appropriately refuted with the *Qur.aan* and the authentic *Sunnah*.

Therefore, it is upon the student of knowledge that he intends by seeking knowledge to advocate the *Sharee'ah*, since this is not possible except by those well-versed in the *Sharee'ah*. Just like weapons; if we had weapons at our disposal that would fill our containers, then would it be possible for these weapons to stand against the enemy and respond to their missiles? Or is this impossible without men?

The answer: This is impossible without men; and such is also the case with knowledge.

Also, innovations are continuously being refashioned, so quite possibly innovations exist which were not present in earlier generations and nor in the books, so it is not possible except for the student of knowledge to refute them, therefore I say:

Certainly, from that which is obligatory for the student of knowledge is adherence to advocating the *Sharee'ah*. Therefore, it is the people who are in dire need of scholars so that they can respond to the deception of the innovators and all of the enemies of Allaah (*Subhaanahu wa Ta'aala*), and this is not possible except with knowledge of the *Sharee'ah* derived from the Book of Allaah and the *Sunnah* of His Messenger (*sal-Allaahu 'alayhi wa sallam*).

4. Tolerance and Patience in Matters of Differences of Opinion

That his heart is most tolerant and patient in matters of differences of opinion which originate from *ijtihaad*. Matters of differences of opinion between the scholars are either from that which there is no scope for *ijtihaad* as the issue is so clear that there is no excuse for anyone to have any difference of opinion; or that there is scope for *ijtihaad* and this provides an excuse for one who has a difference of opinion. Your opinion does not become proof against one who differs with you, because if we were to accept this, then we would also accept the opposite: that his statement is a proof against you.

As for he who differs in opinion to the way of the *Salaf* in such matters as *'aqeedah*, then this difference of opinion is not accepted from anyone. However, in other matters in which there is scope for opinions, then it is not befitting to undertake a verbal attack against those who differ in opinion nor take this as an opportunity to breed hostility and hate.

The Companions (*radhi-yAllaahu 'anhum*) used to differ in opinion in many matters. So those who wish to read about their differences of opinion should refer to those traditions which are available regarding them, and you will find many differences of opinion amongst them. And those issues were greater than that which people differ in these days, such that the people of today adopt *hizbiyyah* by saying: I am with such-and-such and I am with such-and-such, as if the matter is a matter of *hizbiyyah*. Indeed, this is a grave mistake.

For example, one says when rising from the *rukoo'* that you do not place your right hand over your left. Rather, you place your hands by either side, and if you do not do so, then you are a *mubtadi'*.

The term innovator is not easy upon the soul. If someone were to call me an innovator there will develop in my heart some ill feeling, since man is only human. So we say this issue is so open that one may either place them (the right over the left) or let them fall (by either side).

Due to this difference of opinion, *Imaam* Ahmad stipulated a choice between placing one's right hand over the left and letting them fall by either side, because this issue is quite open. However, what is the *Sunnah* in this issue?

The answer: The *Sunnah* is to place the right hand over the left when rising from the *rukoo'* position, just as you place them when you are in the *qiyaam* position. The evidence is what *Imaam* al-Bukhaaree narrated on the authority of Sahl ibn Sa'd who said: *The people were ordered to place the right hand on the left forearm in the prayer.*[9]

Then note, is this what is required in the *sujood* position? Or is it in the *rukoo'* position? Or is it in the *qu'ood* position? No! Rather this is what is required in the *qiyaam*, and that is similar to the *qiyaam* before the *rukoo'* and the *qiyaam* after the *rukoo'*.

So it is obligatory that we do not seek from this difference of opinion between the scholars a reason for disunity and dispute. This is because we all want the truth and are all doing that which we have performed *ijtihaad* for. So, as long as this is the case, then it is not permissible to

---

9 *Saheeh* al-Bukhaaree - The Book of *Salaah*.

take this as a reason for hostility and division between the people of knowledge. This is due to the scholars always differing in opinion, as this was even the case in the time of the Messenger (*sal-Allaahu 'alayhi wa sallam*).

Therefore, it is obligatory upon the students of knowledge to be united and not use differences of opinion as a reason for dividing and bringing about disunity and mutual hatred. Rather, it is obligatory that if you differ with your colleague based upon correct evidence which you have and he too differs with you based upon correct evidence which he has, that you both move towards a single path, whereby you increase in love between yourselves.

Because of this, we love and congratulate our youth who now possess a strong inclination towards linking issues with evidences and basing their knowledge upon the Book of Allaah and the *Sunnah* of His Messenger (*sal-Allaahu 'alayhi wa sallam*). We see this is from the good, and that it bodes well by opening the doors of knowledge from the correct methodologies. We do not want them to make this a cause for partisanship or hatred, as Allaah (*Subhaanahu wa Ta'aala*) said to His Messenger, Muhammad (*sal-Allaahu 'alayhi wa sallam*):

إِنَّ ٱلَّذِينَ فَرَّقُواْ دِينَهُمْ وَكَانُواْ شِيَعًا لَّسْتَ مِنْهُمْ فِى شَىْءٍ

Verily, those who divide their religion and break up into sects, you have no concern in them in the least. [10]

As for those who assemble themselves into parties and band together, then we do not approve of this; because the party of Allaah is one, and

---

10 The Noble *Qur.aan* - *Soorah* al-An'aam, *Aayah* 159.

we see that differing in understanding does not necessitate causing hatred between the people such that one falls on the wrong side of his brother.

So it is obligatory upon the students of knowledge to uphold brotherhood, even if they differ in opinion in some subsidiary issues. It is upon each one to invite the other with calmness and discussion, which is intended for the Sake of Allaah and attainment of knowledge; and this leads to harmony. The harshness and severity in some people causes this to disappear, such that a matter could lead to disagreement and conflict. This, no doubt causes the enemies of *Islaam* much happiness; and conflict within the *Ummah* is from the most severe harm which could befall it, as Allaah (*Subhaanahu wa Ta'aala*) says:

And obey Allaah and His Messenger, and do not dispute lest you lose courage and your strength depart, and be patient. Surely, Allaah is with those who are patient and persevering.[11]

The Companions used to disagree in matters similar to these, but nonetheless they were all united, with true love and harmony. Quite frankly, I say, if a man was to disagree with you on the basis of some evidence he has, then he is really in agreement with you. This is because both of you are in search of the truth, and therefore your goal is one, and that is arriving at the truth by way of evidence. Therefore, he is not in disagreement with you as long as you acknowledge that he is in disagreement

---

11 The Noble *Qur.aan* - *Soorah* al-Anfaal, *Aayah* 46.

with you on the basis of evidence he has. So where is the disagreement? In this manner the *Ummah* will remain as one, despite it disagreeing in some matters based upon evidence it has.

As for he who opposes and is stubborn after the truth has been made clear, then no doubt it is obligatory to deal with him according to what he deserves, as a result of his opposition and disagreement; since every situation has its own particular way of being addressed.

5. Action Based upon Knowledge

That the student of knowledge acts upon the knowledge which he possesses in matters of *'aqeedah*, *'ibaadah*, morals, good manners and dealings with others, because this is the fruit and result of knowledge. And he who possesses knowledge is like he who possesses weapons; it is either for his benefit or destruction. It has been confirmed on the authority of the Prophet (*sal-Allaahu 'alayhi wa sallam*) that he said:

The Qur.aan is proof for you or against you.[12]

It is a proof for you if you acted according to it and a witness against you if you did not act according to it. Likewise, acting according to that which has been authenticated on the authority of the Prophet (*sal-Allaahu 'alayhi wa sallam*), should be in the form of acceptance of the narrations and compliance to the subsequent rulings. So, if some information comes to you from Allaah (*Subhaanahu wa Ta'aala*) and His Messenger (*sal-Allaahu 'alayhi wa sallam*), then accept it (wholeheartedly) in full submission, and do not say why nor how, for certainly, this is the path of the disbelievers, as Allaah (*Subhaanahu wa Ta'aala*) says:

---

12 *Saheeh* Muslim - The Book of Ablution, Chapter - The virtues of ablution.

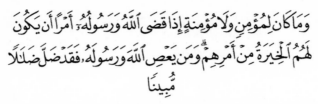

It is not for a believer, man or woman, when Al-laah and His Messenger have decreed a matter that they should have any option in their decision. And whoever disobeys Allaah and His Messenger, he has indeed strayed in a plain error.[13]

As for the Companions, the Prophet (*sal-Allaahu 'alayhi wa sallam*) used to inform them of matters that were sometimes strange and far beyond their comprehension; however, they accepted them and did not say why nor how. This is opposite to what the later generations from this *Ummah* are upon. We find one from amongst them, if a *hadeeth* from the Messenger (*sal-Allaahu 'alayhi wa sallam*) is narrated to him, he begins to analyse it, leading him to reject the statement of the Messenger (*sal-Allaahu 'alayhi wa sallam*) by choice, rather than seek guidance. Thus he separates himself from success, as he rejects that which is narrated on the authority of the Messenger (*sal-Allaahu 'alayhi wa sallam*) because he did not accept it (wholeheartedly) in full submission.

In this case, I offer an example which is confirmed on the authority of the Prophet (*sal-Allaahu 'alayhi wa sallam*), that he said:

Our Lord descends every night to the heaven of this world when the last third of the night is still to come and says, "Who will call on Me so that I may

---

13 The Noble *Qur.aan* - *Soorah* al-Ahzaab, *Aayah* 36.

***answer him? Who will ask Me so that I may give
him? Who will ask forgiveness of Me so that I may
forgive him?"***[14]

This *hadeeth* has been narrated by the Prophet (*sal-Allaahu 'alayhi wa
sallam*) and it is well-known. None of the Companions raised any objec-
tions by saying, 'Oh Messenger of Allaah! How does He descend? And
does He leave His Throne or not?' etc.

However, in this day and age we find some people talking like this and
saying, 'How is He upon His Throne and descending to the lowest heav-
en?' And that which is similar to this from the statements which reject
this, even though they accept this *hadeeth* and say that certainly Allaah
(*Subhaanahu wa Ta'aala*) has risen above His Throne, and His rising is
from that which befits His Majesty, and He descends as He (*Subhaanahu wa Ta'aala*) wishes, just so as to overcome their doubts that they
are not bewildered with that which the Prophet (*sal-Allaahu 'alayhi wa
sallam*) has informed them of their Lord.

Therefore, it is obligatory upon us to accept what Allaah and His Messenger have informed us concerning the matters of the unseen (wholeheartedly), in full submission, and that we do not reject them in favour
of that which is in our minds from our feelings and preconceived no-
tions; because the matters of the unseen are far above this. And examples about this are many, and I do not wish to prolong the issue by
mentioning them. However, the position of the believer when presented
with a hadeeth like this is acceptance in full submission, by saying Allaah
and His Messenger have spoken the Truth, as Allaah informs us in His

---

14 *Saheeh* al-Bukhaaree - The Book of *Tahajjud*;
    Saheeh Muslim - The Book of the Travellers Prayer.

statement:

ءَامَنَ ٱلرَّسُولُ بِمَآ أُنزِلَ
إِلَيْهِ مِن رَّبِّهِۦ وَٱلْمُؤْمِنُونَۚ كُلٌّ ءَامَنَ بِٱللَّهِ وَمَلَـٰٓئِكَتِهِۦ وَكُتُبِهِۦ
وَرُسُلِهِۦ لَا نُفَرِّقُ بَيْنَ أَحَدٍ مِّن رُّسُلِهِۦۚ وَقَالُوا۟ سَمِعْنَا
وَأَطَعْنَاۖ غُفْرَانَكَ رَبَّنَا وَإِلَيْكَ ٱلْمَصِيرُ

The Messenger believes in what has been sent down
to him from His Lord, and the believers. Each one
believes in Allaah, His Angels, His Books, and His
Messengers. They say, "We make no distinction be-
tween one another of His Messengers" - and they
say, "We hear, and we obey. Your Forgiveness, our
Lord, and to You is the return."[15]

Therefore with respect to 'aqeedah, it is obligatory that it is based upon
the Book of Allaah and the *Sunnah* of His Messenger and that the person is aware that there is no scope for the (Islaamically) un-educated
mind in it. I am not saying that there is no scope for the (Islaamically)
educated mind in it, rather, what I am saying is there is no scope for
the (Islaamically) un-educated mind in it, except that which has been
mentioned in the texts with reference to the completeness of Allaah.
Even if the mind does not fully comprehend what is obligatory in respect
to the completeness of Allaah, it comprehends that all the attributes of
completeness have been affirmed for Allaah, and it is imperative that
one acts according to the knowledge of that which Allaah has bestowed
about Himself with respect to 'aqeedah.

---

15 The Noble *Qur.aan* - *Soorah* al-Baqarah, *Aayah* 285.

Also, with respect to *'ibaadah*, then it is only for Allaah (*Subhaanahu wa Ta'aala*), and as is known to many of us, it is based upon two fundamental principles:

Firstly: Sincerity of intention for the Sake of Allaah (*Subhaanahu wa Ta'aala*) alone.

Secondly: Adhering to the *Sunnah* of the Messenger (*sal-Allaahu 'alayhi wa sallam*).

So it is befitting that one should worship upon that which is revealed from Allaah (*Subhaanahu wa Ta'aala*) and (authenticated) from His Messenger (*sal-Allaahu 'alayhi wa sallam*). One must not innovate in the Religion of Allaah that which is not from it; this includes that which is the basis of worship and its manner. Therefore, we say it is imperative that the worship is affirmed in the *Sharee'ah* in all of the following categories with respect to its manner, place, time, and reason/cause.

So, if someone affirmed something as a cause for worship, and worshipped Allaah accordingly without evidence from the *Qur.aan* and *Sunnah*, we reject this from him and say this is unacceptable because it is imperative he affirms this to be a cause for worship based upon evidence, otherwise it is not accepted from him. Also, if one legislated a form of worship which does not occur in the *Sharee'ah*, or he came with something which has been mentioned in the *Sharee'ah*, however its manner has been innovated, or its time has been innovated, we say, certainly this is rejected. This is because it is imperative that worship is based upon that which is mentioned in the *Sharee'ah*, since this is what Allaah (*Subhaanahu wa Ta'aala*) has taught us from the knowledge He has revealed to us, that you do not worship Allaah (*Subhaanahu wa Ta'aala*) except according to that which has been legislated by Him and His Messenger (*sal-Allaahu 'alayhi wa sallam*).

Because of this, the scholars have said the basis for all forms of worship is prohibition until evidence has been established as to it being legislated, and they have based this upon the following statement of Allaah (*Subhaanahu wa Ta'aala*):

$$\text{أَمۡ لَهُمۡ شُرَكَـٰٓؤُا۟ شَرَعُوا۟ لَهُم مِّنَ ٱلدِّينِ مَا لَمۡ يَأۡذَنۢ بِهِ ٱللَّهُ}$$

Or have they partners with Allaah, who have instituted for them a religion which Allaah has not allowed. [16]

And the saying of the Prophet (*sal-Allaahu 'alayhi wa sallam*) in that which has been confirmed on his authority from the *hadeeth* of 'Aa.ishah (*radhi-yAllaahu 'anhaa*):

Anyone who does an act which is not in agreement with us (i.e. Allaah and His Messenger), then he will have it rejected. [17]

Even if you were sincere and wanted to seek the Pleasure of Allaah (*Subhaanahu wa Ta'aala*) and wanted to attain His Honour, if this were not done according to that which has been legislated, then this would be rejected from you. Even if you wanted to seek the Pleasure of Allaah (*Subhaanahu wa Ta'aala*) in a manner which has not been determined by Allaah as a means to seeking His Pleasure, then this is also rejected from you.

---

16 The Noble *Qur.aan* - *Soorah* ash-Shooraa, *Aayah* 21.

17 *Saheeh* Muslim - The Book of Judgements.

Therefore, it is obligatory upon the student of knowledge to worship Al-laah (*Subhaanahu wa Ta'aala*) according to that which he knows from the *Sharee'ah* and not to exceed in this and nor fall short of it. One should not say that this matter in which I wish to worship Allaah is a matter which dwells inside of me, and my heart is at ease and pleased with it. He should not say this in case he attains it, and so it is weighed on the scales of the *Sharee'ah*, and all bodes well if the Book of Allaah and the *Sunnah* are witness to it in terms of acceptance; otherwise his evil act may appear appealing to him (and thus lead him astray) as Allaah (*Subhaanahu wa Ta'aala*) says:

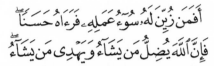

Is he, then, to whom the evil of his deeds is made fairseeming, so that he considers it as good? Verily, Allaah sends astray whom He wills, and guides whom He wills.[18]

It is also imperative he acts according to his knowledge in matters of good behaviour and dealings with others. Knowledge of the *Sharee'ah* calls to all virtuous people in matters of truth, faithfulness and love in all that is good for the believers, such that the Prophet (*sal-Allaahu 'alayhi wa sallam*) said:

None of you truly believes until he loves for his brother what he loves for himself.[19]

---

18 The Noble *Qur.aan* - *Soorah* al-Faatir, *Aayah* 8.

19 *Saheeh* al-Bukhaaree - The Book of *Eemaan*;
    Saheeh Muslim - The Book of *Eemaan*.

And the Prophet (*sal-Allaahu 'alayhi wa sallam*) said:

> **Whoever wishes to be delivered from the Fire and enter the Paradise should die with faith in Allaah and the Last Day and should treat the people as he wishes to be treated by them.**[20]

Many people have a sense of honour and love for the good; however, they do not practice it. For example, we find they are harsh and severe even in the field of *da'wah* to Allaah (*Subhaanahu wa Ta'aala*), and this behaviour is opposite to that which Allaah (*Subhaanahu wa Ta'aala*) has commanded us with.

And know that good behaviour is that by which one gains nearness to Allaah (*Subhaanahu wa Ta'aala*), and the best of the people, and the closest to the Messenger of Allaah (*sal-Allaahu 'alayhi wa sallam*) are those whose degree of good manners are superior, as he (*sal-Allaahu 'alayhi wa sallam*) said:

> **Indeed, the most beloved of you to me and the closest to me on the Day of Judgement are those with the best of manners, and the most detestable to me and furthest away from me on the Day of Judgement are the tharthaaroon (gossip-mongers) and the mutashaddiqoon (ranters and ravers) and the**

---

20 *Saheeh* Muslim - The Book of Principality.

mutafayhiqoon.[21]

His companions said: "O Messenger of Allaah! We know of the *tharthaa-roon* and the *mutashaddiqoon*, so who are the *mutafayhiqoon*?" He said:

The proud ones.

6. The Call to Allaah

That he calls to Allaah (*Subhaanahu wa Ta'aala*) based upon his knowledge, and calls using every possible opportunity: in the *masaajid*, gatherings, in the market places and at all such opportunities. After Allaah (*Subhaanahu wa Ta'aala*) had favoured the Prophet (*sal-Allaahu 'alayhi wa sallam*) with Prophethood and Messengership, he did not sit in his house, rather he used to go out and invite the people to Allaah. Therefore, I do not wish to see the students of knowledge taking to writing books, rather I wish to see them as working students of knowledge, using every opportunity to call to Allaah.

7. Wisdom

That he is distinguished with wisdom, as Allaah (*Subhaanahu wa Ta'aala*) says:

$$ يُؤْتِى ٱلْحِكْمَةَ مَن يَشَآءُ وَمَن يُؤْتَ ٱلْحِكْمَةَ فَقَدْ أُوتِيَ خَيْرًا كَثِيرًا $$

---

21 at-Tirmidhee - The Book of Kindness and Family Ties;
Musnad of *Imaam* Ahmad - Volume 2, Page 189;
Sharhus-Sunnah of al-Baghawee – Volume 12, Page 366;
Mujamma'uz-Zawaa.id of al-Haythamee, where it mentions: Ahmad and at-Tabaraanee narrated it, and the narrators of Ahmad are reliable.

*He grants Hikmah (wisdom) to whom He pleases,
and he, to whom Hikmah is granted, is indeed
granted abundant good.*[22]

Wisdom is that the student of knowledge becomes a teacher of others
with what he possesses of good manners and invites to the Religion of
Allaah (*Subhaanahu wa Ta'aala*), such that he addresses everyone according to that which befits their level of understanding. And if we were
to pursue this path we would acquire much good, as our Lord (*Subhaanahu wa Ta'aala*) says:

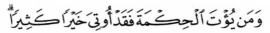

*And he, to whom Hikmah is granted, is indeed
granted abundant good.*[23]

And the *hakeem* is he who adapts matters to their appropriate level;
because the word *hakeem* comes from the word *ihkaam*, and that is
agreement and mastery of a thing whereby he adapts a matter in such a
way as to bring it to its required level. It is therefore befitting, moreover,
obligatory upon the student of knowledge to be wise in his *da'wah*.

Allaah (*Subhaanahu wa Ta'aala*) has mentioned the principles of
da'wah in His (*Subhaanahu wa Ta'aala*) saying:

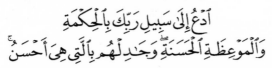

Invite to the Way of your Lord with wisdom and

---

22 The Noble *Qur.aan* - *Soorah* al-Baqarah, *Aayah* 269.

23 The Noble *Qur.aan* - *Soorah* al-Baqarah, *Aayah* 269.

fair preaching, and argue with them in a way that is better.[24]

And Allaah (*Subhaanahu wa Ta'aala*) has mentioned a fourth principle with regards to debating with the People of the Book, by saying:

وَلَا تُجَٰدِلُوٓاْ أَهْلَ ٱلْكِتَٰبِ إِلَّا بِٱلَّتِى هِىَ أَحْسَنُ إِلَّا ٱلَّذِينَ ظَلَمُواْ مِنْهُمْۖ

And argue not with the people of the Scripture, unless it be in that which is better, except with such of them as do wrong.[25]

So the student of knowledge should select from the techniques of giving *da'wah* that which is the closest to acceptance. An example of this is the *da'wah* of the Messenger (*sal-Allaahu 'alayhi wa sallam*); when a Bedouin Arab came and urinated in a part of the *masjid*. The Companions stood to rebuke him, but the Prophet (*sal-Allaahu 'alayhi wa sallam*) forbade them from doing so. When the Bedouin Arab had finished urinating, the Prophet (*sal-Allaahu 'alayhi wa sallam*) called him over and said:

These masaajid are not the places meant for urine and filth; rather, they are only for the remembrance of Allaah, prayer and the recitation of the Qur.aan.[26]

---

24 The Noble *Qur.aan - Soorah* an-Nahl, *Aayah* 125.

25 The Noble *Qur.aan - Soorah* al-'Ankaboot, *Aayah* 46.

26 *Saheeh* al-Bukhaaree - The Book of Ablution;
    Saheeh Muslim - The Book of Purification.

Or the Prophet (*sal-Allaahu 'alayhi wa sallam*) said that which was similar to this.

Have you seen better wisdom than this?

So this Bedouin Arab became so delighted and content that he said: *"O Allaah! Have mercy upon me and Muhammad, and do not be Merciful to anyone else."*

In another story, that of Mu'aawiyah ibn al-Hakam as-Sulamee, who said:

Whilst we were praying with the Messenger of Allaah (sal-Allaahu 'alayhi wa sallam), one of the men sneezed. So I said: "May Allaah have mercy upon you!" So the people all looked at me intensely with piercing eyes. So I said: "What's the matter with you all, looking at me like that?" Then they began beating their thighs with their hands. When I saw them attempting to silence me, I became quiet. When the Messenger of Allaah (sal-Allaahu 'alayhi wa sallam) had finished praying – may Allaah sacrifice my father and my mother for his sake! I have not seen a teacher since better than him. By Allaah! He did not alienate me nor strike me nor insult me, rather he (sal-Allaahu 'alayhi wa sallam) said:

Certainly nothing of the speech of the people is permitted in this prayer, rather, that which is permitted is the glorification and proclamation of the Greatness of Allaah and the reciting of the Qur. aan. [27]

---

27 *Saheeh* Muslim - The Book of *Masaajid* and the Places of Prayer.

And from this, we find it is obligatory to undertake the *da'wah* to Allaah with wisdom as Allaah (*Subhaanahu wa Ta'aala*) has commanded.

And yet another example is when the Prophet (*sal-Allaahu 'alayhi wa sallam*) saw a man and on his hand he had a gold ring, and the gold ring is *haraam* (prohibited) for the men. So the Prophet (*sal-Allaahu 'alayhi wa sallam*) took it off his hand and threw it away, then said:

2

> ***One of you is wishing for live coal from Hell, and putting it on his hand.***[28]

So when the Prophet (*sal-Allaahu 'alayhi wa sallam*) left, it was said to the man: *"Take your gold ring and derive benefit from it"* (i.e. sell it). So he said: *"No! By Allaah, I will not take it when Allaah's Messenger (sal-Allaahu 'alayhi wa sallam) has thrown it away."*

So the manner of advising here is more severe, since every situation has its own particular way of being addressed. Similarly, it is befitting for everyone who invites to the Path of Allaah to adapt accordingly to the level of the one he is calling and not to consider all the people on one or the same level; since the desired result is to achieve benefit for all concerned.

If we carefully consider that which many of the *du'aat* are upon today, we find some of them are overcome by enthusiasm and as a result cause offence, such that the people have an aversion to their call.

If they find someone doing something which is *haraam*, they make a very big thing of it and forcefully say: *"Don't you fear Allaah?"* or some-

---

28 *Saheeh* Muslim - The Book of Clothing.

thing similar to this, such that the person has an aversion to them, and this is not good because this is dealing with the issue in the manner which is completely opposite to that which is correct.

When *Shaykh* al-Islaam ibn Taymiyyah was transmitting on the authority of *Imaam* ash-Shaafi'ee about that which he saw from the *Ahlul-Kalaam*, he said: *"My ruling as regards the Ahlul-Kalaam is to beat them with branches (stripped of their leaves) and shoes, and to parade them around the tribes and to say this is the reward of those who leave the Book and the Sunnah, and accept kalaam."*

Shaykh al-Islaam ibn Taymiyyah said: *"If a person looks at these people he finds them from one angle, most worthy of that which Imaam ash-Shaafi'ee has said; however, if he looks at them from the point of qadar and freedom of will, then they are overcome by this (that which has been written for them), and the Shaytaan possesses them; thereby the person sympathises and shows compassion towards them. He asks Allaah to protect him from that which they have been afflicted with, since they have been given intelligence and have not been given uprightness, or they have been given understanding and have not been given knowledge, or they have been given hearing, sight and hearts; so of no benefit have their hearing, sight or hearts been to them."*

Like this dear brothers, it is befitting that we look at the sinful people from two viewpoints: the point of *Sharee'ah* and the point of *qadar*.

As for from the point of *Sharee'ah*, then we are not taken to account for blaming the blameworthy, as Allaah (*Subhaanahu wa Ta'aala*) says with regard to the adulterer and the adulteress:

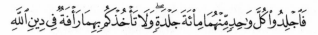

فَٱجْلِدُواْ كُلَّ وَٰحِدٍ مِّنْهُمَا مِائَةَ جَلْدَةٍ وَلَا تَأْخُذْكُم بِهِمَا رَأْفَةٌ فِي دِينِ ٱللَّهِ

...flog each of them with a hundred stripes. Let not pity withhold you in their case, in a punishment prescribed by Allaah.[29]

And then we look at them from the point of *qadar*. So we show sympathy and compassion towards them and deal with them according to that which is closest to achieving that which is required and alleviating that which is disliked.

And this is from the traits of a student of knowledge as opposed to one who has no knowledge and is ignorant and over-enthusiastic. So it is obligatory for the student of knowledge who calls to the Path of Allaah to use wisdom.

8. The Student of Knowledge is Patient in Seeking Knowledge

That he is patient and persevering in seeking knowledge, and that he does not cease and nor does he become bored, rather he is consistent in seeking knowledge according to his ability.

He should be patient in seeking knowledge and not become bored, for certainly, when boredom strikes a person, it persists to such an extent that he becomes tired and weary, and then ultimately ceases this noble act.

However, if he is patient and persevering in seeking knowledge, then from one angle he will certainly attain the reward of the patient ones,

---

29 The Noble *Qur.aan - Soorah* an-Noor, *Aayah* 2.

while from another angle it will be an achievement for him. Pay attention to the saying of Allaah (*Subhaanahu wa Ta'aala*) addressing His Prophet (*sal-Allaahu 'alayhi wa sallam*):

This is of the news of the unseen which We reveal unto you, neither you nor your people knew them before this. So be patient. Surely, the end is for the Muttaqoon (pious).[30]

9. Respecting the Scholars and their Positions

It is upon the students of knowledge to respect and appreciate the scholars and to accommodate in their hearts any differences of opinion which may occur between them and other than them. And to deal with this by giving an excuse to one who pursues the wrong path based upon what he believes. This is a very important point, because some people follow the mistakes of others, taking from that which is not befitting of their rights, thereby confusing the people regarding the scholars' standing. And this ranks amongst the greatest of mistakes; if backbiting of the layman ranks amongst the major sins, then backbiting of the scholar is much greater. This is because the effect of backbiting of the scholar does not rest at him only; rather it rests upon him <u>and</u> that which he possesses in knowledge of the *Sharee'ah*.

If the people renounce a scholar; or if he has fallen in their eyes, then the same will be the case with regard to his words. If he speaks the truth

---

30 The Noble *Qur.aan - Soorah* Hood, *Aayah* 49.

and guides to it, then the backbiting of this scholar becomes an obstacle between the people and his knowledge of the *Sharee'ah*. And its dangers are great and considerable.

Certainly, I say it is upon the youth to accept that which passes between the scholars from differences of opinion with good intention, and upon *ijtihaad* and to offer excuses in that which they err in.

And there is no harm in speaking to them about that which you consider they have erred in, so as to clarify whether this error is directly from them or from those who say they have erred. This is because a person sometimes assumes that the statement of the scholar is a mistake, then, after discussing it the truth is made clear to him. And man is only human, as the Messenger of Allaah (*sal-Allaahu 'alayhi wa sallam*) has said:

> ### All of the children of Aadam make mistakes, and the best of them are those who repent.[31]

As for taking delight in the lapse of the scholar and his mistake so as to

---

31 *Musnad* of *Imaam* Ahmad - Volume 3, Page 198;

at-Tirmidhee - The Book of the description of the Day of Judgement, Volume 4, Page 569, No.2499;

Ibn Maajah - The Book of Abstention;

ad-Daarimee - The Book of *ar-Riqaaq*;

Sharhus-Sunnah of al-Baghawee — Volume 5, Page 92;

al-Hilyah of Abu Na'eem - Volume 6, Page 332;

Kashful-Khafaa of al-Ajloonee. - Volume 2, Page 120;

al-Mustadrak of al-Haakim - Volume 4, Page 273, where it mentions: This *hadeeth* has a sound chain of narrators and they (al-Bukhaaree and Muslim) have not transmitted it;

Sharhus-Sunnah of al-Baghawee - Volume 2, Page 120 where it mentions: Its chain of narrators is strong.

circulate this amongst the people to cause division, then this is certainly not from the way of the *Salaf*.

This is also the case with the errors of the leaders; it is impermissible for us to take that which they err in as an opening to speak evil of them in everything and to overlook their good deeds, as Allaah (*Subhaanahu wa Ta'aala*) says in His Book:

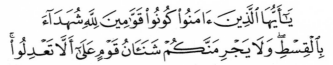

O you who believe! Stand out firmly for Allaah and be just witnesses and let not the enmity and hatred of others make you avoid justice.[32]

In other words, you cannot bear the aversion of a people over and above their lack of honesty. Therefore honesty is obligatory, and it is not permissible for a person to take the mistakes of any one of the leaders or the scholars or others besides them and then circulate them amongst the people, whilst remaining silent about their good deeds. Certainly, this is not honesty!

Consider yourself: just imagine for a moment that someone in authority over you went about spreading your mistakes and bad deeds and screening your good deeds. Certainly, you would regard this as a serious crime against you. So, if you can see this regarding yourself then it is obligatory upon you to see the same for others besides yourself. Just as I have mentioned previously, the cure to that which you suspect to be a mistake is to telephone the one whom you suspect has made the mis-

---

32 The Noble *Qur.aan* - *Soorah* al-Maa.idah, *Aayah* 8.

take and discuss the issue with him, then consider your position <u>after</u> the discussion.

So how many people, after the discussion has taken place revert from their opinions to that which is the correct one? And how many people, after the discussion has taken place have found their opinion to be the correct one, whilst we suspected him to be in error?

The Messenger of Allaah (*sal-Allaahu 'alayhi wa sallam*) said:

> ***A faithful believer to a faithful believer is like the bricks of a wall, enforcing each other.***[33]

While saying that the Prophet (*sal-Allaahu 'alayhi wa sallam*) clasped his hands by interlacing his fingers.

And the Messenger of Allaah (*sal-Allaahu 'alayhi wa sallam*) also said:

> ***Whoever wishes to be delivered from the Fire and enter the Paradise should die with faith in Allaah and the Last Day and should treat the people as he wishes to be treated by them.***[34]

And this is what is regarded as honesty and uprightness.

---

33 *Saheeh* al-Bukhaaree - The Book of the *Masaajid*;
    Saheeh Muslim - The Book of Kindness and Family Ties.

34 *Saheeh* Muslim - The Book of Principality.

10. Holding Steadfast to the *Qur.aan* and the *Sunnah*

It is obligatory upon the students of knowledge to adhere strictly to seeking knowledge from authentic sources; without which there is no success. And these are:

1. The Noble *Qur.aan*: It is obligatory upon the student of knowledge to adhere strictly to reading, memorising, understanding and acting according to it. Certainly, the *Qur.aan* is the strong and firm rope of Allaah and it forms the basis for all Islaamic knowledge. The *Salaf* used to adhere strictly to it, making this their goal.

In mentioning something astonishing about their strict adherence to the *Qur.aan*, you would find one of them had memorised the *Qur.aan* by the age of seven years, whilst others had memorised the *Qur.aan* in less than a month. In this there is a clear sign regarding the strict adherence to the *Qur.aan* by the *Salaf* (*radhi-yAllaahu 'anhum*). It is therefore obligatory upon the student of knowledge to adhere strictly to it and memorise it under the guardianship of one of its teachers, because the *Qur.aan* is memorised through being instructed by a qualified teacher.

It is regretful that one finds some of the students of knowledge do not memorise the *Qur.aan*, nor do they seek proficiency in its reading, and this is a great shortcoming in their approach. Because of this, I reiterate that it is obligatory upon the students of knowledge to adhere strictly to memorising the *Qur.aan* and act according to it and invite to it and understand it according to the understanding of *as-Salaf as-Saalih*.

2. The Authentic Sunnah: This is the second of the two sources of the *Sharee'ah*, and it is the expounder of the Noble *Qur.aan*. So, it is obligatory upon the student of knowledge to combine the two and strictly adhere to them both. And it is also upon the student of knowledge to memorise the *Sunnah*, either by memorising the *nusoos* of the *ahaa-deeth* or by studying the *asaaneed* and its *mutoon*, and differentiating the *saheeh* from the *da'eef*. Likewise, memorising the *Sunnah* is done by protecting it and refuting the doubts of the innovators of the *Sunnah*.

So it is obligatory upon the student of knowledge to adhere strictly to the *Qur.aan* and the authentic *Sunnah*, because they are for him like two wings of a bird: if one of them becomes damaged then it is unable to fly.

Because of this, do not adhere to the *Sunnah* and be neglectful of the *Qur.aan*, nor adhere to the *Qur.aan* and be neglectful of the *Sunnah*; because many of the students of knowledge devote their total attention to the *Sunnah* and its exegeses and knowledge of its narrators and its technical terms. However, if you were to ask him about a verse from the Book of Allaah you will find him to be completely ignorant of it, and this is a great mistake. Therefore it is imperative for the *Qur.aan* and the *Sunnah* to be two wings for you O student of knowledge.

Here I would like to mention a third and very important matter, and that is the statements of the scholars. Do not overlook and be neglectful of the statements of the scholars, because the scholars are more firm and steadfast than you in knowledge, since they possess knowledge of the rules of the *Sharee'ah* and its principles; quite simply, that which you do not possess.

It is therefore obligatory upon the student of knowledge to resort to the Book of Allaah and the *Sunnah* of His Messenger (*sal-Allaahu 'alayhi wa sallam*) and make use of the statements of the scholars.

Resorting to the Book of Allaah is done by memorising it and reflecting over it and acting according to it, because Allaah (*Subhaanahu wa Ta'aala*) says:

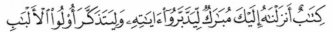

A Book which We have sent down to you, full of blessings that they may ponder over its verses, and that men of understanding may remember.[35]

That they may ponder over its verses.

So reflecting upon the verses will lead to an understanding of their meanings.

وَلِيَتَذَكَّرَ أُوْلُوا الْأَلْبَبِ

And that men of understanding may remember.

And remembrance is acting in accordance to the *Qur.aan*.

This is the wisdom with which the *Qur.aan* has been revealed. Since this is the case, then let us turn to it to reflect over and understand its meanings, implementing that which it mentions, for certainly by Allaah, there is the welfare of this world and the Hereafter in it, as Allaah (*Subhaanahu wa Ta'aala*) says:

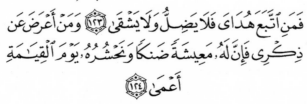

---

35 The Noble *Qur.aan* - *Soorah* Saad, *Aayah* 29.

Then whoever follows My Guidance shall neither go astray, nor fall into distress and misery. But whosoever turns away from My Reminder verily, for him is a life of hardship, and We shall raise him up blind on the Day of Resurrection.[36]

Because of this, you will never find anyone more blessed with clear thought, peace and tranquillity in his heart than the believer; even if he is poor and destitute. Therefore, amongst the people the believer is the one who is most full of happiness, and most peaceful and tranquil, and the most blessed with clear thought. So read the statement of Allaah (*Subhaanahu wa Ta'aala*):

مَنۡ عَمِلَ صَٰلِحٗا مِّن ذَكَرٍ
أَوۡ أُنثَىٰ وَهُوَ مُؤۡمِنٞ فَلَنُحۡيِيَنَّهُۥ حَيَوٰةٗ طَيِّبَةٗ وَلَنَجۡزِيَنَّهُمۡ
أَجۡرَهُم بِأَحۡسَنِ مَا كَانُوا۟ يَعۡمَلُونَ

Whoever works righteousness, whether male or female, while he is a true believer verily, to him We will give a good life, and We shall pay them certainly a reward in proportion to the best of what they used to do.[37]

What is the good life?

The answer: The good life is the inner delight and peace of heart, such that if one was in the worst of affairs, he would still be cheerful and at

---

36 The Noble *Qur.aan* - *Soorah* Taa-Haa, *Aayah*s 123-124.

37 The Noble *Qur.aan* - *Soorah* an-Nahl, *Aayah* 97.

81

peace in his heart. The Prophet (*sal-Allaahu 'alayhi wa sallam*) said:

> **Strange are the ways of a believer for there is good in every affair of his and this is not the case with anyone else except in the case of a believer; for if he has an occasion to feel delight, he thanks (Allaah), thus there is good for him in it, and if he gets into trouble and shows resignation (and endures it patiently), there is good for him in it.**[38]

If the *kaafir* was afflicted with adversity, would you find him to be patient?

<u>The answer</u>: No! Rather, he would be sad and find the world around him has tightened. Quite possibly he may revert to committing suicide, whilst on the other hand the believer is patient and finds the sweet taste of patience and is cheerful and tranquil. As a result, his life discovers good, and with that, he benefits as Allaah (*Subhaanahu wa Ta'aala*) says:

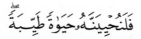

Verily, to him We will give a good life.[39]

That is, the good life is in having a contented heart and soul.

Some of the historians have spoken about the life of *al-Haafiz* Ibn Hajar (*rahima-hullaah*). He was a judge from amongst the judges of Egypt in

---

38 *Saheeh* Muslim - The Book of Abstention.

39 The Noble *Qur.aan* - *Soorah* an-Nahl, *Aayah* 97.

his time, and he would go to his place of work riding in a carriage being pulled by horses or mules in a caravan. So one day, he passed by a Jewish man who sold oil; and from the traits of one who sells oil is that his clothing would often be dirty, so the Jewish man approached the caravan and halted it. And he said to *al-Haafiz* Ibn Hajar (*rahima-hullaah*), *"'Verily your Prophet used to say:*

The world is a prison for a believer and a paradise for a non-believer.[40]

You are a judge from amongst the judges of Egypt, and you are in this caravan, in this ease and comfort, whilst I am in this affliction and suffering!'"

al-Haafiz Ibn Hajar (*rahima-hullaah*) said to him: *"I am in that which I am, of ease and comfort, in comparison to the ease and comfort of Paradise, a prison. And as for you, with respect to the suffering which you are in, according to the Fire of Hell, is Paradise."*

The Jewish man then said: *"I testify, there is none truly worthy of worship except Allaah, and I testify that Muhammad is the Messenger of Allaah."* And thus he accepted Islaam.

So a believer is in good fortune in whichever situation he finds himself in, and he is the one who gains from this world and the Hereafter.

And the *kaafir* is in misfortune and is a loser in this world and the Hereafter.

---

40 *Saheeh* Muslim - The Book of Abstention.

Allaah (*Subhaanahu wa Ta'aala*) says:

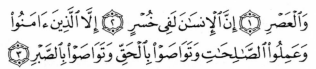

By al-'Asr (the time). Verily! Man is in loss, Except those who believe and do righteous good deeds, and recommend one another to the truth, and recommend one another to patience.[41]

Therefore, the *kaafir* and those having neglected the Religion of Allaah and sought ease in their pleasure and comfort, will discover that even if they built palaces and their worldly life prospered, certainly in reality they are in hell. In response, some of the *Salaf* used to say: *"If the kings and the kings' children knew that which we were in, they would quarrel with us over it with swords."*

As for the believers, then they are taking pleasure in the intimate discourse of Allaah and His remembrance, and are under the decree of Allaah and His predestination. If they are subjected to any harm, they are patient, and if they are subjected to any pleasure, they are thankful, and they are amongst the most blessed in that which is possible. This is quite opposite to the pleasure seekers of this world, for verily they are as described by Allaah (*Subhaanahu wa Ta'aala*):

$$فَإِنْ أُعْطُوا مِنْهَا رَضُوا وَإِن لَّمْ يُعْطَوْا مِنْهَا إِذَا هُمْ يَسْخَطُونَ$$

If they are given part thereof, they are pleased,

---

41 The Noble *Qur.aan - Soorah* al-'Asr, *Aayahs* 1-3.

84

***but if they are not given thereof, behold! They are
enraged!*[42]**

As for resorting to the *Sunnah* of the Prophet (*sal-Allaahu 'alayhi wa
sallam*), then the *Sunnah* of the Messenger (*sal-Allaahu 'alayhi wa
sallam*) is established and preserved before us, and all praise is for Allaah, even that which is fabricated concerning the Messenger of Allaah
(*sal-Allaahu 'alayhi wa sallam*). Certainly, the people of knowledge
have explained his *Sunnah*, and have explained that which has been
fabricated concerning him, such that the *Sunnah* is clear and preserved,
and all praise is for Allaah. Further, one is able to gain access to it either
by referring to the books, if that is possible, or else by questioning the
people of knowledge.

However, if a person says: "How do you reconcile between what you
have said with regards to resorting to the Book of Allaah and the *Sunnah*
of His Messenger (*sal-Allaahu 'alayhi wa sallam*), taking into account
that we find the people are adhering to the books compiled by the differing *madhaahib* and they say: *'I belong to such and such a madhhab,'*
*'And me, I belong to such and such a madhhab,' 'As for me, well I belong
to such and such a madhhab?'* Such that you pass a religious verdict for
the man and say to him: 'The Prophet (*sal-Allaahu 'alayhi wa sallam*)
said such and such,' he will say: *'I am a Hanafee,'* or, *'I am a Maalikee,'*
or, *'I am a Shaafi'ee,'* or, *'I am a Hanbalee,'* or the like?!"

The answer: That we say to them, we all say:

---

42 The Noble *Qur.aan - Soorah* at-Tawbah, *Aayah* 58.

أَشْهَدُ أَلَّا إِلَهَ إِلَّا الله،

وَ أَشْهَدُ أَنَّ مُحَمَّداً رَسُوْلُ الله

I testify, there is none truly worthy of worship except Allaah alone, and I testify that Muhammad is the Messenger of Allaah.

Then, what is the meaning of the testification that Muhammad is the Messenger of Allaah?

The scholars have said its meaning is: Adhering to that which he has commanded, and attesting to that which he has informed about, and avoiding that which he has prohibited and deterred from, and not to worship Allaah except according to what has been legislated.

So if one was to say: *"I adhere to such and such a madhhab,"* or, *"I am with such and such a madhhab,"* then we say to him: *"This is the saying of the Messenger (sal-Allaahu 'alayhi wa sallam), so do not contradict it with the saying of anyone else!"*

Even the scholars of the *madhhabs* have prohibited their pure and sheer blind following, and they have said[43]: *"Whenever the truth is made clear, then it is obligatory to resort to it."*

So we say to the one who is objecting concerning the *madhhab* of such and such: *"We both testify that Muhammad is the Messenger of Allaah,*

---

43 <u>Translator's Note</u>: I refer the reader to Appendix I, quoting from the book "The Prophet's Prayer Described" by the Noble Scholar and *Muhaddith*, *Shaykh* Muhammad Naasirudden al-Albaanee (*rahima-hullaah*) on this subject.

and this testification requires that we do not follow anyone except the Messenger of Allaah (sal-Allaahu 'alayhi wa sallam). This is the Sunnah before us, plain and clear."

However, by this statement I do not mean that we should belittle the importance of referring to the books of the jurists and the people of knowledge. Rather, one should refer to their books to seek benefit and understanding of the methods they applied in deriving the rulings from their evidences; since this is not possible for the student of knowledge to achieve except by referring to them.

Because of this, we find those people who do not study with the scholars have a serious number of errors. This is because they begin contemplating to a lesser degree than that which is befitting to contemplate with, such that they take *Saheeh* al-Bukhaaree for example, and begin looking up *ahaadeeth*. We know amongst the *ahaadeeth* there are those which are *'aam* and those which are *mukhassas*, whilst there are those which are *mutlaq* and those which are *muqayyad*, and those which are *mansookh*; however they have as yet to be guided to all this. Therefore, without this knowledge they begin to stray in a very serious manner.

11. Verification and Firmness

From amongst the most important disciplines which are obligatory for the student of knowledge to possess is verification; verification in transmitting news and verification in passing judgement. So, if information is transmitted, then it is imperative to verify its authenticity from the one whom it is being transmitted. If it is authenticated, and a religious verdict is issued, then quite possibly the information you have heard may be based upon a principle which you are unaware of, leading you to pass judgement that the religious verdict is a mistake; whilst in reality it is not a mistake!

So what is the remedy for such a situation?

The remedy is that you must call the one to whom this news is attributed and say to him, *"Such and such has been transmitted on your authority, is this correct?"* Then, discuss the issue with him. It could be that your disagreement and subsequent alienation of him was due to what you heard, which was alarming because you do not know the reason for that which has been transmitted.

It is said: *"If the reason is known, then there is no alarm."* So, it is imperative to firstly verify the information and religious verdict, thereafter, call the one from whom it is being transmitted and ask him: *"Has this been authenticated or not?"* Then discuss it with him; either it will be that he is upon the truth and that which is correct, so you turn to it, or that which you are upon is the truth, so he will turn to it, *inshaa.-Allaah*.

There is a difference between *thabaat* and *tathabbut*, and they are two words which are linguistically similar, yet differ in meaning.

As for *thabaat*, then it implies patience and perseverance and not to become tired nor bored and not to take a little from each and every book, nor take a little from each and every subject then leave it, as this harms the student of knowledge by wasting away days without benefit.

For example, some students study the subject of *nahoo*; sometimes they refer to the text of الآجُرُومِيَّة then to قَطْرُ النَّدَى and then to أَلْفِيَّةُ بْنُ مَالِك. This is also the case with *mustalah al-hadeeth*; sometimes they refer to نُخْبَةُ الْفِكر and sometimes to أَلْفِيَّةُ العِرَاقِي. And this is also the case with *fiqh*; sometimes they refer to زَادُ الـــمُسْتَقْنِع, sometimes to عُمْدَةُ الْفِقه, at other times they refer to الـــمُغْنِي and then to شَرْحُ الـــمُهَذَّب.

Such is the case with all the various topics and their books. Generally, this does not assist in seeking knowledge, and even if it does, then all that has been covered are (secondary) issues and not the principles. Acquiring the (secondary) issues is similar to the one who catches a locust - one after the other; however, that which is important to possess is the qualities of *ta.seel*, *rusookh* and *thabaat*.

So have *thabaat* with regard to the books which you read or refer to, and also *thabaat* with regard to the scholars from whom you seek knowledge. Do not be like the one who goes to a different scholar every week, nor one who goes to another scholar every month; but instead, decide from which scholar you wish to seek knowledge, then, when you have decided, make firm your decision. Do not be undecided and go to different scholars every week or every month. There is no harm in you taking a scholar for *fiqh* and continuing with him in this; another scholar in nahoo and continuing with him in this; and yet another scholar in *'aqeedah* and *tawheed* and continuing with him in this. The important thing is to continue and persevere, and not be undecided and drift from one scholar to another. This is like the man who is a persistent divorcer; whenever he marries a woman, he spends some days with her then divorces her and then goes and finds another!

Also, *tathabbut* is an important matter because the transmitters sometimes have evil intentions. They deliberately transmit that which aims to discredit the transmission; sometimes they do not have evil intentions, but nevertheless, they understand a matter contrary to that which was intended. Because of this, it is obligatory to seek *tathabbut*. So if the chain of narration serves to verify that which is transmitted, you arrive at a level of discussion with the one from whom it is being transmitted before you pass judgement on the statement that it is a mistake or not. This is because it may quite possibly become clear to you after the discussion that the truth is really with the one from whom the statement is transmitted.

In conclusion, if a statement is transmitted on the authority of such-and-such, and you feel it is wrong, then adhere to the following three steps, in order:

Firstly: Verify the authenticity of the narration;

Secondly: Look into the issue to ascertain the correct ruling; if it is correct, then support and uphold the position of the one from whom the narration is transmitted. However, if you find it is wrong, then proceed to step three;

Thirdly: Telephone the one from whom the narration is transmitted and discuss the issue with him calmly and respectfully.

12. Taking Care to Understand the *Qur.aan* and the *Sunnah*

From among the matters which are important in seeking knowledge is the issue of understanding, i.e. understanding that which was intended by Allaah (*Subhaanahu wa Ta'aala*) and His Messenger (*sal-Allaahu 'alayhi wa sallam*).

This is because many people have knowledge, but they do not have the understanding. It is not enough just to memorise the Book of Allaah and that which is easy from the *Sunnah* of the Messenger of Allaah (*sal-Allaahu 'alayhi wa sallam*) without understanding them. It is imperative to understand that which was intended by Allaah (*Subhaanahu wa Ta'aala*) and His Messenger (*sal-Allaahu 'alayhi wa sallam*). What greater failing is there than those who draw conclusions using evidences from the Book of Allaah and the *Sunnah* of His Messenger (*sal-Allaahu 'alayhi wa sallam*), contrary to what was intended by Allaah (*Sub-*

90

haanahu wa Ta'aala) and His Messenger (*sal-Allaahu 'alayhi wa sallam*), thereby leading them to deviation?

Here, I wish to make a very important point, and that is:

A mistake through lack of understanding can often be more dangerous than a mistake through ignorance.

This is because the ignorant is he who makes mistakes based upon his ignorance and knows he is ignorant, but nonetheless is learning.

Whilst he who misunderstands believes himself to be most learned and correct; believing such-and-such is what Allaah (*Subhaanahu wa Ta'aala*) and His Messenger (*sal-Allaahu 'alayhi wa sallam*) have intended. We offer a few examples here to clarify the importance of understanding:

Example One:

Allaah (*Subhaanahu wa Ta'aala*) says:

وَدَاوُۥدَ وَسُلَيۡمَٰنَ إِذۡ يَحۡكُمَانِ فِي ٱلۡحَرۡثِ إِذۡ
نَفَشَتۡ فِيهِ غَنَمُ ٱلۡقَوۡمِ وَكُنَّا لِحُكۡمِهِمۡ شَٰهِدِينَ ﴿٧٨﴾
فَفَهَّمۡنَٰهَا سُلَيۡمَٰنَ وَكُلًّا ءَاتَيۡنَا حُكۡمٗا وَعِلۡمٗا وَسَخَّرۡنَا
مَعَ دَاوُۥدَ ٱلۡجِبَالَ يُسَبِّحۡنَ وَٱلطَّيۡرَ وَكُنَّا فَٰعِلِينَ ﴿٧٩﴾

And Daawood and Sulaymaan, when they gave judgement in the case of the field in which the sheep of certain people had pastured at night and We were witness to their judgement. And We made

Sulaymaan to understand, and to each of them We gave Hikmah and knowledge. And We subjected the mountains and the birds to glorify Our Praises along with Daawood. And it was We Who were the doers. [44]

Allaah (*Subhaanahu wa Ta'aala*) has, from the aspect of understanding, preferred Sulaymaan (*'alayhis-salaam*) over Daawood (*'alayhis-salaam*) in this particular case, as Allaah (*Subhaanahu wa Ta'aala*) says:

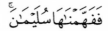

And We made Sulaymaan to understand. [45]

However, there is no deficiency in the knowledge of Daawood (*'alayhis-salaam*), as Allaah (*Subhaanahu wa Ta'aala*) says:

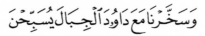

And to each of them We gave Hikmah and knowledge. [46]

Look at this *aayah* where Allaah (*Subhaanahu wa Ta'aala*) has distinguished Sulaymaan (*'alayhis-salaam*) with understanding and He (*Subhaanahu wa Ta'aala*) has also distinguished Daawood (*'alayhis-salaam*), as He (*Subhaanahu wa Ta'aala*) says:

وَسَخَّرْنَا مَعَ دَاوُدَ ٱلْجِبَالَ يُسَبِّحْنَ

---

44 The Noble *Qur.aan* - *Soorah* al-Anbiyaa., *Aayah*s 88-89.

45 The Noble *Qur.aan* - *Soorah* al-Anbiyaa., *Aayah* 89.

46 The Noble *Qur.aan* - *Soorah* al-Anbiyaa., *Aayah* 89.

And We subjected the mountains and the birds to
glorify Our Praises along with Daawood.[47]

That is so both of them can be equal. So Allaah (*Subhaanahu wa Ta'aala*) has mentioned that which both of them shared in wisdom and knowledge, and then He (*Subhaanahu wa Ta'aala*) mentioned that which each is distinguished with over the other.

This demonstrates for us the importance of understanding, and that knowledge is not everything.

Example Two:

Supposing you had two containers, one in which there was hot water and the other in which there was very cold water. It was winter time, and you wanted to take a *ghusl* due to the *janaabah*. Some people would say it is preferable to use the cold water because there is much hardship in it; since the Messenger of Allaah (*sal-Allaahu 'alayhi wa sallam*) said:

Should I not suggest to you that by which Allaah obliterates the sins and elevates the ranks (of man)?[48]

They said: "Yes, Messenger of Allaah." He said:

Performing the ablution thoroughly despite the odds.

---

47 The Noble *Qur.aan - Soorah* al-Anbiyaa., *Aayah* 89.

48 *Saheeh* Muslim, The Book of Purification.

What this means is to perform the *wudoo* properly in the cold days. So, if you performed *wudoo* with cold water, it is superior to performing *wudoo* with warm water which is naturally more appropriate to the weather. So, the man passes a religious verdict that the use of cold water is superior and has drawn this conclusion using the evidence from the previous *hadeeth*.

So is the error in the knowledge or the understanding?

<u>The answer</u>: Certainly the error is in the understanding, because the Messenger of Allaah (*sal-Allaahu 'alayhi wa sallam*) said:

Performing the ablution thoroughly despite the odds.[49]

And he (*sal-Allaahu 'alayhi wa sallam*) did not say that you choose the cold water for *wudoo*, so there is a difference between the two expressions. If the second expression was reported in the *hadeeth*, we would say yes, choose the cold water. However, he (*sal-Allaahu 'alayhi wa sallam*) said:

Performing the ablution thoroughly despite the odds.

i.e. the use of cold water does not prevent one from performing *wudoo*.

Then, we say, does Allaah (*Subhaanahu wa Ta'aala*) intend ease for His servants or does He (*Subhaanahu wa Ta'aala*) intend hardship for

---

49 *Saheeh* Muslim, The Book of Purification.

them?

The answer: The saying of Allaah (*Subhaanahu wa Ta'aala*):

يُرِيدُ اللَّهُ بِكُمُ الْيُسْرَ وَلَا يُرِيدُ بِكُمُ الْعُسْرَ

Allaah intends for you ease, and He does not
want to make things difficult for you.[50]

And in the saying of the Prophet (*sal-Allaahu 'alayhi wa sallam*):

Indeed, the religion is easy.

So I say to the students of knowledge: certainly the issue of understanding is an important issue, and it is upon us to understand what Allaah has intended for His servants. Did He (*Subhaanahu wa Ta'aala*) intend hardship for them in performing their acts of worship or did He intend ease for them?

Certainly, there is no doubt that Allaah (*Subhaanahu wa Ta'aala*) intended ease and not hardship for us.

And these are just some of the important disciplines which are obligatory for the student of knowledge to possess, thus influencing his knowledge so that he becomes a competent example and such that he becomes a caller to that which is good and a leader in the Religion of Allaah (*Subhaanahu wa Ta'aala*). So, it is with patience and certainty that one attains leadership in the Religion, as Allaah (*Subhaanahu wa Ta'aala*) says:

---

50 The Noble *Qur.aan* - *Soorah* al-Baqarah, *Aayah* 185.

وَجَعَلْنَا مِنْهُمْ أَئِمَّةً يَهْدُونَ
بِأَمْرِنَا لَمَّا صَبَرُواْ وَكَانُواْ بِـَٔايَٰتِنَا يُوقِنُونَ

And We made from among them, leaders, giving guidance under Our command, when they were patient and used to believe with certainty in Our Aayaat.[51]

---

51 The Noble *Qur.aan* - *Soorah* as-Sajdah, *Aayah* 24.

Part Two

Means Which Assist in Acquiring Knowledge

2

The means which assist in acquiring knowledge are many; from amongst them we mention (the following):

1. *Taqwa* - Fear of Allaah and Devotion to Him

This is the Recommendation of Allaah conveyed to the early and later generations amongst His servants, as Allaah (*Subhaanahu wa Ta'aala*) says:

وَلَقَدْ وَصَّيْنَا ٱلَّذِينَ أُوتُواْ ٱلْكِتَبَ
مِن قَبْلِكُمْ وَإِيَّاكُمْ أَنِ ٱتَّقُواْ ٱللَّهَ وَإِن تَكْفُرُواْ فَإِنَّ لِلَّهِ
مَا فِى ٱلسَّمَوَتِ وَمَا فِى ٱلْأَرْضِ وَكَانَ ٱللَّهُ غَنِيًّا حَمِيدًا

And verily, We have recommended to the people of the Scripture before you, and to you that you fear Allaah, and keep your duty to Him, But if you disbelieve, then unto Allaah belongs all that is in the heavens and all that is in the earth, and Allaah is

Ever Rich, Worthy of all praise. [1]

And this is also the recommendation of the Messenger of Allaah (*sal-Allaahu 'alayhi wa sallam*) for his nation, as Abu Umaamah Sadaa ibn 'Ajlaan al-Baahalee (*radhi-yAllaahu 'anhu*) said:

"'I heard the address of the Prophet (sal-Allaahu 'alayhi wa sallam) on the occasion of the Last Pilgrimage in the course of which he said:

> **Fear your Lord, observe the five (daily prayers), fast the month (of Ramadhaan); pay the zakaah (poor due) and obey those in authority among you (except when they order you to commit sin); you will then enter the Paradise of your Lord.'"** [2]

When the Messenger of Allaah (*sal-Allaahu 'alayhi wa sallam*) used to dispatch a detachment of *Sahaabah* he used to advise their leader to fear Allaah, and those with him from amongst the Muslims, to do good.

And likewise, the *Salaf* continued to advise the people to fear Allaah in their *khutbah*s, their writings and their legacies at death.

'Umar ibn al-Khattaab (*radhi-yAllaahu 'anhu*) wrote to his son 'Abdullaah: *"To proceed: Certainly I advise you to fear Allaah (Subhaanahu wa Ta'aala), for he who fears Him, then He protects him, and he who asks of Him, then He rewards him with it, and he who thanks Him, then He increases him in it."*

---

1 The Noble *Qur.aan - Soorah* an-Nisaa., *Aayah* 131.

2 at-Tirmidhee, The Book of *Jumu'ah*.

Likewise, 'Alee ibn Abee Taalib (*radhi-yAllaahu 'anhu*) advised a man saying: *"I advise you to fear Allaah (Subhaanahu wa Ta'aala) Whom it is inevitable you are to meet, and there is no limit for you without Him, and He possesses this world and the Hereafter."*

And one of the pious people wrote to one of his Muslim brothers: *"To proceed: I advise you to fear Allaah Who will safeguard your inner-most thoughts, and Who is a Watcher over your outward actions. So appoint Allaah over all your affairs from the night and the day. So fear Allaah according to His nearness to you and according to His Power over you, and know that with His Sight you never leave His Sovereignty for another or from His Dominion to another. And He will increase your awareness and fear of Him and shall safeguard you."*

And the meaning of *taqwa*: That the servant assigns between himself and that which he fears a safeguard which will protect him from it.

And the *taqwa* of the servant of His Lord: That the servant assigns between himself and that which he is in awe of and reverence to, a safeguard which will protect him from His Anger and His Displeasure by doing that which is in obedience to Him and avoiding that which is in disobedience to Him.

And know that *taqwa* is often related to *birr*, so it is said *birr* and *taqwa* just as Allaah (*Subhaanahu wa Ta'aala*) says:

$$وَتَعَاوَنُواْ عَلَى ٱلْبِرِّ وَٱلتَّقْوَىٰ$$

Help you one another in al-Birr and at-Taqwa.[3]

---

3 The Noble *Qur.aan - Soorah* al-Maa.idah, *Aayah* 2.

And sometimes it is mentioned singly; so if *taqwa* is coupled with *birr*, then *birr* becomes the doing of that which has been obligated and *taqwa* being leaving that which has been prohibited.

If it is singled out, then it encompasses the doing of that which has been obligated and leaving that which has been prohibited; as Allaah (*Subhaanahu wa Ta'aala*) has mentioned in His Book that *Jannah* has been prepared for the *muttaqeen*, so those who have *taqwa* are the people of Paradise – may Allaah make us all from amongst them! Because of this, it is obligatory upon the person to fear Allaah (*Subhaanahu wa Ta'aala*) in obedience of His Commands and seeking His Reward and salvation from His Punishment. Allaah (*Subhaanahu wa Ta'aala*) says:

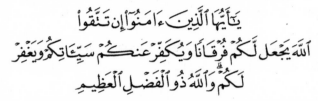

O you who believe! If you obey and fear Allaah, He will grant you Furqaan (a criterion) and will expiate for you your sins, and forgive you, and Allaah is the Owner of the Great Bounty.[4]

Within this *aayah* are three very important points of benefit:

First Point of Benefit: Allaah (*Subhaanahu wa Ta'aala*) says:

يَجۡعَل لَّكُمۡ فُرۡقَانࣰا

---

4 The Noble *Qur.aan* - *Soorah* al-Anfaal, *Aayah* 29.

He will grant you Furqaan (a criterion).[5]

i.e. He will grant you that which will assist you in distinguishing the truth from the falsehood, and the harmful from the beneficial. Included in this category is knowledge which Allaah reveals to a person that which He does not reveal to any other. So *taqwa* is a means to attaining increased guidance, knowledge and memorisation; because of this, we quote the following from *Imaam* ash-Shaafi'ee (*rahima-hullaah*):

2

> *'I complained to Wakee'*[6] *about my poor memory;*
> *So he advised me to abandon sins.*
> *And he said: "Know that knowledge is light,*
> *And the Light of Allaah is not bestowed upon the sinner."'*

There is no doubt, the more a person increases in knowledge, naturally he increases in learning and differentiating the truth from the falsehood, and the harmful from the beneficial, and like this he reaches a level whereby Allaah reveals understanding to him. This is because *taqwa* is a means for strengthening understanding, and strong understanding assists in increasing knowledge. So you see two men memorising an *aayah* from the Book of Allaah; one of them can extract from it three rulings, whilst the other is able to extract more than this, according to that which Allaah has blessed him with in understanding.

So *taqwa* is a means for increasing knowledge; also included in this is insight. Allaah has blessed the *muttaqee* with insight with which he is able to distinguish even amongst the people.

---

5 The Noble *Qur.aan - Soorah* al-Anfaal, *Aayah* 29.

6 Translator's Note: Wakee' ibn al-Jarraah who died in the year 196 A.H. was one of the famous scholars of the *Salaf*; he was also the teacher of *Imaam* ash-Shaafi'ee.

So, from simply seeing a person he is able to know whether he is honest or dishonest, or pious or obscene, such that it is possible he is able to judge a person whom he has not met and does not know anything about him because of what Allaah has blessed him with in terms of insight.

<u>Second Point of Benefit</u>: Allaah (*Subhaanahu wa Ta'aala*) says:

And will expiate for you your sins.[7]

Expiation of evil deeds is done by good actions, since good actions expiate evil deeds, as the Prophet (*sal-Allaahu 'alayhi wa sallam*) said:

> *The five daily prayers, and from one Jumu'ah prayer to the next Jumu'ah prayer, and from fasting one Ramadhaan to fasting the next Ramadhaan is an expiation for that which occurs between them, so long as the major sins are avoided.*[8]

And the Messenger of Allaah (*sal-Allaahu 'alayhi wa sallam*) also said:

> *The performance of an 'Umrah to the performance of the next 'Umrah is an expiation for that which occurs between them.*[9]

So the expiation is by good actions; this means that if a person fears Al-

---

7 The Noble *Qur.aan* - *Soorah* al-Anfaal, *Aayah* 29.

8 *Saheeh* Muslim - The Book of Purification.

9 *Saheeh* al-Bukhaaree - The Book of *'Umrah*;
   Saheeh Muslim - The Book of *Hajj*.

laah, Allaah will make it easy for him to do good actions with which he can make expiation.

<u>Third Point of Benefit</u>: Allaah (*Subhaanahu wa Ta'aala*) says:

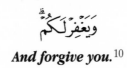

And forgive you. [10]

i.e. that Allaah will make easy the seeking of forgiveness and repentance, for this is certainly a blessing of Allaah upon the servant.

2. Perseverance and Consistency in Seeking Knowledge

It should be pointed out to the student of knowledge that he must make every effort in obtaining knowledge and be patient whilst doing so, and to protect and preserve it once he has attained it. Certainly, knowledge is not acquired with ease and comfort. So the seeker pursues all the paths leading to knowledge and with that he is rewarded, as is confirmed in an authentic narration that the Prophet (*sal-Allaahu 'alayhi wa sallam*) said:

> *Whoever treads a path in search of knowledge, Allaah will make easy for him the Path to Paradise.* [11]

The student of knowledge must persevere and exert himself, and stay awake at night and pray to Allaah (*Subhaanahu wa Ta'aala*) to relieve

---

10 The Noble *Qur.aan* - *Soorah* al-Anfaal, *Aayah* 29.

11 *Saheeh* al-Bukhaaree: Chapter - Knowledge precedes Speech and Action;
   Saheeh Muslim - The Book of Invitations;
   Musnad Imaam Ahmad.

him of all that preoccupies him from seeking knowledge.

There are well-known examples about the *Salaf* regarding perseverance in seeking knowledge, such as that narrated on the authority of Ibn 'Abbaas (*radhi-yAllaahu 'anhu*), who was asked about how knowledge is attained. He said: "*With a questioning tongue, an intelligent and wise heart, and a healthy body.*"

It is also narrated on his authority (*radhi-yAllaahu 'anhu*) that he said: "*A narration about a man reached me, so I went to his house. I waited at his door and the wind was blowing sand upon me. Upon answering the door he said: 'O son of the uncle of the Messenger of Allaah, what brings you here? Had you sent for me I would have come to you!'*" *So Ibn 'Abbaas (radhi-yAllaahu 'anhu) said: "It is more befitting that I come to you, and so I asked him about the narration.*"

Ibn 'Abbaas (*radhi-yAllaahu 'anhu*) was humble in seeking knowledge, so Allaah raised his rank.

Like this, it is befitting for the student of knowledge to display immense perseverance, such as that which is narrated regarding *Imaam* ash-Shaafi'ee (*rahima-hullaah*), when he was a guest of *Imaam* Ahmad one night. Supper was placed before him so *Imaam* ash-Shaafi'ee ate. Afterwards, the two men departed to their sleeping quarters. *Imaam* ash-Shaafi'ee remained awake thinking about extracting rulings from a particular *hadeeth*; the saying of the Prophet (*sal-Allaahu 'alayhi wa sallam*):

O Abu 'Umayr! What did the nughayr do?[12]

---

12 *Saheeh* al-Bukhaaree - The Book of Manners.

Abu 'Umayr had a small bird which he had named *an-nughayr*. So when the bird died the young child grieved over it.

As is known, the Prophet (*sal-Allaahu 'alayhi wa sallam*) responded to him, just as he used to play and jest with the young children, he used to speak to each and every individual according to that which was appropriate to them.

So *Imaam* ash-Shaafi'ee continued the entire night in extracting rulings from this *hadeeth*; and it has been said that he managed to extract more than one thousand points of benefit. It was possible that he deduced one point of benefit which prompted him to another *hadeeth* and like this he continued until he finished, such that when the *adhaan* (call to prayer) for *Salaatul-Fajr* was made, *Imaam* ash-Shaafi'ee (*rahima-hullaah*) rose and did not make ablution, and then left for his house. *Imaam* Ahmad praised him within his family, so they said to him: "*O Abu 'Abdullaah, how is it you praise this man who ate and drank and then slept and did not stand the night in prayer, and then performed Salaatul-Fajr without ablution?*"

So *Imaam* Ahmad questioned *Imaam* ash-Shaafi'ee, who said: "*As for my having eaten until I had finished what was put before me, that was because I had not found food which tasted better than the food of Imaam Ahmad, so I wanted to fill my belly with it. And as for my not having stood the night in prayer, then the seeking of knowledge is better than standing the night in prayer as I was busy pondering over a hadeeth. And as for my having not made ablution for Salaatul-Fajr, then I was already in a state of ablution from Salaatul-'Ishaa.*"

And this is also because he did not wish to inconvenience them for water to renew his ablution.

In any case, perseverance in seeking knowledge is an important matter; so we look at ourselves today, do we have such perseverance? No! As for those who study under the education system, then when they finish their lessons perhaps they pass their time with things which do not assist them in their studies. I offer an example, the like of which I hope does not occur:

One of the students in a lesson answered rudely, so the teacher asked him: *"Why?"*

And the student said: *"Because I have given up hope of understanding this subject, so I do not study it. However, I want to attain a certificate in the subject."*

Why such loss of hope?

This is a major mistake. It is obligatory that we persevere until we reach our goal.

As my *Shaykh*, the persevering 'Abdur-Rahmaan as-Sa'dee (*rahima-hullaah*) related to me about al-Kisaa.ee, who was the *Imaam* of the people of Koofah in Arabic grammar. He sought knowledge in Arabic grammar but was not able to achieve this. So one day, he saw an ant carrying some food for itself whilst climbing a wall. Each time it climbed up, it fell; however, it persevered until it had rid itself of the difficulty and finally scaled the wall. So al-Kisaa.ee said: *"This ant persevered until it reached its goal."* So he himself persevered until he became a scholar in Arabic grammar.

Therefore, it is befitting for us, O students of knowledge, that we persevere and we do not lose hope, for verily losing hope means shutting the door to good. And it is befitting for us that we are not pessimistic, rather we are optimistic and that we turn ourselves to that which is good.

3. Memorising and Preserving

It is obligatory upon the student of knowledge to adhere to revise and verify that which he learns, either by memorising it by heart or by writing it, since man is only human and is liable to forget. If he does not adhere to continuous revision and repetition of that which he learns, then this will lead him to forget and ultimately lose what he has learnt.

It has been said:

> *'Knowledge is a "hunting game" (which is sought),*
> *and writing is the way to "catch" (attain) it.*
> *So it is from foolishness to hunt a gazelle,*
> *and thereafter leave it to perish.'*

What is implied is that writing is the ideal method by which one gains knowledge and it would be foolish to simply seek knowledge without writing, as this knowledge will ultimately be lost.

From the ways which assist in memorising knowledge and verifying it, is that the person follows the right path with the knowledge he has. As Allaah (*Subhaanahu wa Ta'aala*) says:

$$وَٱلَّذِينَ ٱهۡتَدَوۡاْ زَادَهُمۡ هُدٗى وَءَاتَىٰهُمۡ تَقۡوَىٰهُمۡ$$

While as for those who accept guidance, He increases their guidance, and bestows on them their piety. [13]

---

13 The Noble *Qur.aan* - *Soorah* Muhammad, *Aayah* 17.

And He (*Subhaanahu wa Ta'aala*) says:

وَيَزِيدُٱللَّهُٱلَّذِينَٱهۡتَدَوۡاۡهُدٗى

And Allaah increases in guidance those who walk aright.[14]

So, the more a person does an action according to his knowledge, Allaah (*Subhaanahu wa Ta'aala*) increases him in his ability to memorise and understand, as He (*Subhaanahu wa Ta'aala*) says:

زَادَهُمۡ هُدٗى

He increases their guidance.[15]

4. Accompanying the Scholars

It is obligatory upon the student of knowledge to seek assistance from Allaah (*Subhaanahu wa Ta'aala*), then from the people of knowledge, in addition to seeking assistance from that which the people of knowledge have written in their books; Because confining oneself to reading alone requires a lot of time, which is contrary to sitting with a scholar who explains and sheds light upon matters for him.

I am not saying he will not attain knowledge except by taking from the scholars, since a person is able to attain knowledge by reading and researching; however, in most cases if he does not persevere day and night and is not blessed with understanding, then he is liable to make many mistakes, and because of this it is said:

---

14 The Noble *Qur.aan* - *Soorah* Maryam, *Aayah* 76.

15 The Noble *Qur.aan* - *Soorah* Muhammad, *Aayah* 17.

> *'One whose guide is his book, then his mistakes*
> *are more prevalent than him being correct.'*

Having said this, in reality this is not always the case.

However, the most exemplary way is to take knowledge from the scholars. I also advise the student of knowledge not to "grab" from every scholar, knowledge of the same subject. For example, to study *fiqh* with more than one scholar, since the scholars differ in their techniques of inference from the *Qur.aan* and the *Sunnah*, and they also differ in their opinions. So assign yourself a scholar from whom you can take knowledge in *fiqh* or *balaaghah* and the like, i.e. take knowledge in one subject from one scholar. If the scholar has more than one field of knowledge, then continue with him, for if you took knowledge of *fiqh* for example from such-and-such and then such-and-such, and they differed in their opinions, what would be your position since you are still a student?! Your position would be that of confusion and doubt! However, your continuance with one scholar in a particular subject will lead to peace of mind, *inshaa.-Allaah*.

Chapter Three

Paths to acquiring knowledge
and mistakes against which precautions must be taken.

Within this chapter there are two parts:

Part One
Paths to Acquiring Knowledge

Part Two
Mistakes against which Precautions Must Be Taken

Part One

Paths to Acquiring Knowledge

3

From that which is known is that if a person wanted to get to a place, then it is imperative he knows the way to reach it, and if there are many ways, then he will search for the shortest and easiest way. Because of this, it is important for the student of knowledge to base his search for knowledge on principles and not to beat around in the darkness (of ignorance); for he who is not well-versed in the principles is prevented from reaching his goal, as the poet says:

> *To proceed: Knowledge is a vast ocean,*
> *(and) the seeker will never attain all of it.*
> *However, in (learning) the principles there is*
> *ease in attaining it,*
> *so take care and you will find a way.*
> *Learn the rules and principles, since he who does*
> *not is prevented from arriving at the goal.*

So the principles are the knowledge, and the issues are the branches; just like the foundation of the tree and its branches. If the branches are not upon a firm foundation, they will wither and ultimately perish. However, what are the principles? Are they the authentic proofs? Or are they rules? Or are they both?

The principles are the proofs from the *Qur.aan* and the *Sunnah* and the rules that are obtained by following and studying them. These are from amongst the most important for the student of knowledge. For example, "hardship gives way to ease," and this is from the principles that are extracted from the *Qur.aan* and the *Sunnah*.

In the *Qur.aan*, Allaah (*Subhaanahu wa Ta'aala*) says:

And He has not laid upon you in religion any hardship.[1]

And from the *Sunnah*, the saying of the Messenger of Allaah (*sal-Allaahu 'alayhi wa sallam*) to 'Imraan ibn Husayn:

Perform your prayer standing, and if you are unable to do so, then sitting down, and if you are unable to do so, then lying down on your side.[2]

And the Messenger of Allaah (*sal-Allaahu 'alayhi wa sallam*) also said:

If I have ordered you to do something, then do that which you are able to do.[3]

If a thousand different issues were put forward for you to pass judge-

---

1 The Noble *Qur.aan* - *Soorah* al-Hajj, *Aayah* 78.

2 *Saheeh* al-Bukhaaree - The Book of Shortening the Prayer;
   Saheeh Muslim - The Book of the Travellers Prayer and it's Shortening.

3 *Saheeh* al-Bukhaaree - The Book of Adherence (to Allaah and His Messenger);
   Saheeh Muslim - The Book of *Hajj*.

ment upon, then it is possible for you to do so based upon this principle. However, if you did not have knowledge of this principle, and a couple of issues were put forward to you, then they would all be a cause of difficulty for you.

So there are two ways to acquiring knowledge:

1. Referring to reliable books

That you take from reliable books, and particularly those which have been written by scholars known for their knowledge and trustworthiness, and sound *'aqeedah* - being free from any form of innovations and deviations. It is imperative that the person, in taking knowledge from books, reaches the goal he set out for. However, in this there are two obstacles:

The first obstacle: That the person requires a lot of time and tough endurance and great effort so that he reaches that which he is aiming for in his search for knowledge. Often, many people do not give importance to this obstacle, especially since they see they have wasted much time without benefit. Therefore, laziness overcomes them and they become exhausted and bored such that they are unable to attain that which they set out for.

The second obstacle: That he who takes his knowledge simply from books, then his knowledge is mostly weak. It is not built upon principles or rules. As a result of this, we find he has many mistakes. This is because he does not possess any principles or rules upon which he is able to build the different aspects of knowledge which are found in the *Qur. aan* and the *Sunnah*.

We find some people refer to a *hadeeth* which is not mentioned in the authentic books of *hadeeth*, and this manner is contrary to that which is from the authentic principles dictated by the people of knowledge. Then he takes this *hadeeth* and bases his *'aqeedah* upon it. Without a doubt this is a mistake, because the *Qur.aan* and the *Sunnah* have principles upon which the different aspects of knowledge are based. Thus, it is imperative to refer these different aspects of knowledge to principles; so that if we find anything from them which is conflicting with these principles, such that it is not possible to arrive at a consensus, then we leave these different aspects of knowledge.

2. Referring to a reliable teacher

From the ways to acquiring knowledge is that you take from a teacher who is reliable in his knowledge and religion, and this is the fastest and most reliable manner for seeking knowledge. As with the first approach the student is open to deviation while he does not know, either because of his lack of understanding or inadequate knowledge or other than these reasons.

As for the second approach, then here there is constructive discussion whilst taking knowledge and refuting (doubts) with the teacher. With this, many doors of understanding, verification and methods of safeguarding the authentic statements and refuting the weak statements, are opened for the student. If the student was to combine the two approaches then this is more perfect and complete.

So, the student of knowledge begins with that which is important and then moves on in order of importance. He starts with the short texts of knowledge before moving onto the extended full-length texts. He progresses from level to level, and does not progress to the next level until he is fully versed in the preceding level, such that his progression is sound and complete.

Part Two

Mistakes against which Precautions Must Be Taken

3

There are mistakes which some of the students of knowledge fall into, and amongst them are:

1. Jealousy and Envy

It is to dislike that which Allaah has blessed one of His servants with. It is not just a desire for the cessation of that which Allaah has blessed other than him with; rather it is absolute dislike of the person for that which Allaah has blessed him with over and above someone else. And this is jealousy and envy, irrespective of whether it is a desire for its cessation or for it remaining whilst he dislikes him.

Just as has been affirmed by *Shaykh* al-Islaam Ibn Taymiyyah (*rahima-hullaah*) who said: *"Jealousy and envy is disliking a person for that which Allaah has blessed him with over and above others."*

Often jealousy will not leave the inner soul, meaning that it becomes compulsive within the soul. However, it has been mentioned in a *hadeeth*:

***If you become jealous, then do not intend it; and
if you become suspicious, then do not seek it out.***[1]

Meaning, that it is obligatory upon a person, should he notice jealousy
in his heart for another, that he does not offend him with any statement
or action, for certainly that is from the practice of the Jews, about whom
Allaah (*Subhaanahu wa Ta'aala*) says:

أَمْ يَحْسُدُونَ ٱلنَّاسَ عَلَىٰ مَآ ءَاتَىٰهُمُ ٱللَّهُ مِن فَضْلِهِۦ فَقَدْ
ءَاتَيْنَآ ءَالَ إِبْرَٰهِيمَ ٱلْكِتَٰبَ وَٱلْحِكْمَةَ وَءَاتَيْنَٰهُم مُّلْكًا عَظِيمًا

***Or do they envy men for what Allaah has given
them of His Bounty? Then We had already given
the family of Ibraaheem the Book and alHikmah
(asSunnah), and conferred upon them a great
kingdom.***[2]

Then the jealous one falls into many prohibitions:

<u>Firstly</u>: His disliking that which Allaah (*Subhaanahu wa Ta'aala*) has
decreed, for certainly, disliking that which Allaah (*Subhaanahu wa
Ta'aala*) has blessed someone with is to dislike that which Allaah has
decreed. This constitutes opposing the ruling of Allaah (*Subhaanahu
wa Ta'aala*).

---

1 Fat.h al-Baaree of *al-Haafiz* Ibn Hajar – Volume 10, Page 213;
   at-Tamheed of Ibn 'Abdul-Barr – Volume 6, Page 125;
   al-Kabeer of at-Tabaraanee – Volume 3, Page 8258;
   Kashf al-Khafaa. of 'al-'Ajaloonee – Volume 1, Page 104;
   Tafseer al-Qur.aan al-'Adtheem of Ibn Katheer – Volume 4, Page 191.

2 The Noble *Qur.aan - Soorah* an-Nisaa., *Aayah* 54.

<u>Secondly</u>: Jealousy devours the good deeds, just as fire devours wood; for in most cases the jealous one is prepared for his victim with mention of that which he dislikes by frightening the people away from the victim, and putting him down in that which he is able. And this is from amongst the major sins which could possibly outweigh one's good deeds.

<u>Thirdly</u>: That which settles in the heart of the jealous one, in the form of grief and the burning "fire" which devours him, such that each time Allaah bestows a blessing upon his victim, he becomes distressed and his chest tightens. He observes this person, and in all that Allaah has blessed him with, he is saddened and distressed and the world around him tightens.

3

<u>Fourthly</u>: Certainly in jealousy there is a likening to the Jews, and that which is known is that he who involves himself in a practice of the disbelievers becomes one of them in this act, as the Prophet (*sal-Allaahu 'alayhi wa sallam*) said:

> ***Whoever resembles a people (nation); then he is (considered to be) from amongst them.***[3]

---

3 Musnad of *Imaam* Ahmad – Volume 5, Page 5;
   Abu Daawood – The Book of Clothing;
   al-Musannaf of Ibn Abee Shaybah – Volume 5, Page 313;
   Mujamma'uz-Zawaa.id of al-Haythamee – Volume 10, Page 271;
   at-Tamheed of Ibn 'Abdul-Barr – Volume 6, Page 80
   Majmoo' al-Fataawa of Ibn Taymiyyah – Volume 5, Page 331, where it mentions: Its *isnaad* is good.
   Fat.h al-Baaree of *al-Haafiz* Ibn Hajar – Volume 6, Page 97;
   al-Jaami' as-Sagheer of as-Suyootee – Volume 1, Page 590;
   Ahmad Shaakir has authenticated the *hadeeth* in *al-Musnad*, number 5114.

<u>Fifthly</u>: Jealousy conflicts with the completeness of *eemaan*, as the Prophet (*sal-Allaahu 'alayhi wa sallam*) has said:

> ***None of you truly believes until he wishes for his brother what he wishes for himself.***[4]

This means that you dislike for the cessation of a blessing of Allaah upon another, and if you do not dislike this then you do not love for your brother that which you love for yourself, and this conflicts with the completeness of *eemaan*.

<u>Sixthly</u>: Jealousy results in the turning away of the servant from asking Allaah (*Subhaanahu wa Ta'aala*) of His Favours; so you find him always concerned with the blessing which Allaah has bestowed upon other than him, and subsequenty, he fails to ask Allaah of His Favours, as He (*Subhaanahu wa Ta'aala*) said:

وَلَا تَتَمَنَّوْاْ مَا فَضَّلَ ٱللَّهُ بِهِۦ بَعْضَكُمْ عَلَىٰ بَعْضٍ لِّلرِّجَالِ نَصِيبٌ مِّمَّا ٱكْتَسَبُواْ وَلِلنِّسَآءِ نَصِيبٌ مِّمَّا ٱكْتَسَبْنَ وَسْـَٔلُواْ ٱللَّهَ مِن فَضْلِهِۦٓ

And wish not for the things in which Allaah has made some of you to excel others. For men there is reward for what they have earned, for women there is reward for what they have earned, and ask Allaah of His Bounty.[5]

---

4 *Saheeh* al-Bukhaaree - The Book of *Eemaan*.

5 The Noble *Qur.aan* - *Soorah* an-Nisaa., *Aayah* 32.

<u>Seventhly</u>: Jealousy leads to contempt of the blessing of Allaah upon him. Meaning, that the jealous one sees he is not in any blessing, and the victim is in a blessing greater than him, and as a result, despises the blessing of Allaah upon himself and does not turn to express gratitude, but instead becomes neglectful.

<u>Eighthly</u>: Jealousy is an ugly characteristic. The jealous one observes the blessings of Allaah upon someone from amongst his group, then he attempts, with all he is able to muster, to interfere amongst the people and the victim by putting him down in that which he is able. He does this by scorning at that which the victim attempts in doing good as well as other things.

<u>Ninthly</u>: That the jealous one, when he becomes jealous of his victim, often resorts to attacking him; in this case, his victim will take from his good deeds on the Day of Judgement, and if there are no good deeds remaining, the jealous one will take from the evil deeds of the victim, such that he will finally be hurled into the hellfire.

<u>Summary</u>: Certainly jealousy is an ugly characteristic, and sadly it is more prevalent amongst the scholars and the students of knowledge, and amongst the merchants too. Indeed, anyone who has a trade, then his opponent is jealous of him. However, it is more predominant amongst the scholars and the students of knowledge. This is sad, particularly since it is more appropriate and befitting for the people of knowledge to be the furthest from jealousy and the nearest to the perfection of good morals and ethics.

My dear brother, if you see that Allaah has blessed one of his servants with something, then strive hard to be like him. Do not dislike him whom Allaah has blessed with something, rather say:

اللّٰهُمَّ زِدْهُ مِنْ فَضْلِكَ وَ أَعْطِنِي أَفْضَلَ مِنْهُ

*O Allaah increase for him from your favours and
grant me better than him.*

And jealousy does not change a thing from the state of the victim; however, as we have just mentioned in these causes of corruption and evil and the nine dangers listed, hopefully, he who reflects over them will find much to ponder over, and Allaah is the One from Whom assistance is sought.

2. Passing a Religious Verdict without Sound Knowledge

Passing religious verdicts is a great rank; with it, one who is qualified is able to deal with issues that are uncertain for the general public in matters of their religion, that which guides them to the Straight Path. Since this is such a great rank, no-one should put themselves forward for it unless they are qualified to do so. Therefore, it is obligatory for the servants of Allaah to fear Him and not speak except upon sound knowledge.

Know that He is the Creator and all matters are at His disposal. So there is no creator except Allaah; there is no planner for the creation except Allaah, and there is no law for the creation except the Law of Allaah. So it is He Who obligates and prohibits things, just as He is the One Who permits things. Allaah has rebuked those who make things *halaal* and *haraam* based upon their whims and desires as He (*Subhaanahu wa Ta'aala*) says:

قُلْ أَرَءَيْتُم مَّا أَنزَلَ ٱللَّهُ لَكُم مِّن رِّزْقٍ فَجَعَلْتُم مِّنْهُ حَرَامًا وَحَلَٰلًا قُلْ ءَآللَّهُ أَذِنَ لَكُمْ أَمْ عَلَى ٱللَّهِ تَفْتَرُونَ ۝ وَمَا ظَنُّ ٱلَّذِينَ يَفْتَرُونَ عَلَى ٱللَّهِ ٱلْكَذِبَ يَوْمَ ٱلْقِيَٰمَةِ

Say: "Tell me, what provision Allaah has sent down to you! And you have made of it lawful and un-lawful." Say: "Has Allaah permitted you, or do you invent a lie against Allaah?" And what think those who invent lies against Allaah, on the Day of Resurrection?[6]

As He (*Subhaanahu wa Ta'aala*) also says:

وَلَا تَقُولُوا لِمَا تَصِفُ أَلْسِنَتُكُمُ ٱلْكَذِبَ هَٰذَا حَلَٰلٌ وَهَٰذَا حَرَامٌ لِّتَفْتَرُوا۟ عَلَى ٱللَّهِ ٱلْكَذِبَ إِنَّ ٱلَّذِينَ يَفْتَرُونَ عَلَى ٱللَّهِ ٱلْكَذِبَ لَا يُفْلِحُونَ ۝ مَتَٰعٌ قَلِيلٌ وَلَهُمْ عَذَابٌ أَلِيمٌ ۝

And say not concerning that which your tongues put forth falsely: "This is lawful and this is forbid-den," so as to invent lies against Allaah. Verily, those who invent lies against Allaah will never prosper. A passing brief enjoyment, but they will have a painful torment.[7]

---

6 The Noble *Qur.aan - Soorah* Yoonus, *Aayah*s 59-60.

7 The Noble *Qur.aan - Soorah* an-Nahl, *Aayah*s 116-117.

Certainly from amongst the greatest sins is for a person to say something is halaal or haraam while he does not know Allaah's (*Subhaanahu wa Ta'aala*) Judgement upon it. Or he says something is *waajib* while he does not know that Allaah has made it *waajib*, or he says something is *ghayr waajib* while he does not know that Allaah has made it *ghayr waajib*. Certainly, these are serious offences and ill-manners towards Allaah (*Subhaanahu wa Ta'aala*).

How is it O servant of Allaah, that you know the judgement is for Allaah alone and you put yourself forward before Him and say about His Religion and His Law that which you do not know? Allaah has linked such a statement without knowledge to *shirk* (associating partners with Him), as He (*Subhaanahu wa Ta'aala*) says:

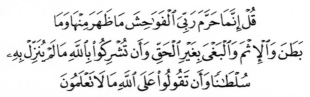

Say: "The things that my Lord has indeed forbidden are al-Fawaahish (great evil sins) whether committed openly or secretly, sins, unrighteous oppression, joining partners with Allaah for which He has given no authority, and saying things about Allaah of which you have no knowledge."[8]

Many amongst the general Muslims pass religious verdicts about that which they do not know. So you find them saying such-and-such is *halaal* or *haraam*, or *waajib* or *ghayr waajib*, while they know absolutely nothing about it!

---

8 The Noble *Qur.aan* - *Soorah* al-A'raaf, *Aayah* 33.

Do they not know that Allaah (*Subhaanahu wa Ta'aala*) is going to question them about that which they have said, on the Day of Judgement?

Do they not know if they misguide someone by making something *halaal* while Allaah has made it *haraam*, or making something *haraam* while Allaah has made it *halaal*, that they draw themselves to his sins and upon them is the burden of that which he does, and that is as a result of what they passed as a religious verdict for him?

There are some who commit yet another offence. If they see someone who wants to seek the judgement of a scholar, they say to him there is no need to seek the judgement of a scholar, since the matter is quite clear that it is *haraam*, while in actual fact it is *halaal* (or vice versa).

3

So he makes *haraam* that which Allaah has made *halaal*, or he says to him this is *waajib* and obligates upon him that which Allaah has not obligated, or he says this is *ghayr waajib*, while it is *waajib*; thereby relieving him of that which Allaah has obligated upon him, or he says this is *halaal* when in actual fact it is *haraam*.

His offence is against the Law of Allaah and deception against his Muslim brother since he has passed a religious verdict without sound knowledge.

Have you seen when someone asks you directions to a place, and you say the way is from here while in actual fact you do not know; will the people not consider this to be deception on your part? Then how do you speak about the way to *Jannah* which is the Law Allaah has revealed while you know nothing about it?!

And certainly some of the teachers are but small fish compared to the scholars, since they fall into that which the general Muslim has fallen into by way of audacity in matters of making something *halaal* and *haraam*, or *waajib* and the like. So they talk about that which they do not know, and they generalise the *Sharee'ah* and categorise it, while they are amongst the most ignorant people with regard to the Judgement of Allaah. If you were to hear one of them speak, it is as if revelation were descending upon him in that which he is saying with absolute authority and lack of caution. Is it not possible for him to say: I do not know, with the fact that lack of knowledge is one of his true and confirmed attributes? However, he insists, based upon his ignorance, that he is knowledgeable. So as a result he harms the general Muslims, because perhaps the people have trust in what he is saying and are being deceived by him.

If only these people confined themselves to that which is of real concern to them. Instead, you see them ascribing to *Islaam* that which they do not know, and then saying *Islaam* says such-and-such, and views such-and-such. This is not permissible, except for that which the speaker knows is from the Religion of Islaam. There is no cure for this except by knowing and understanding the Book of Allaah and the *Sunnah* of His Messenger (*sal-Allaahu 'alayhi wa sallam*) and the consensus of the Muslims upon it.

Certainly, some of the people, because of their audacity, lack of piety, modesty and their lack of fear of Allaah, say regarding something which is clearly *haraam*, *"I do not think it is haraam,"* or regarding something which is clearly *waajib*, *"I do not think it is waajib."* This is either as a result of their ignorance about it; their stubbornness and obstinacy; or causing doubt for the servant of Allaah regarding the Religion of Allaah.

O brothers, certainly it is from common sense and *eemaan* and from the fear of Allaah that a man says regarding that which he does not know

— *"I have no knowledge,"* or *"I do not know,"* or *"Ask other than me,"* for certainly this is from the completeness of common sense. This is because if the people saw him to be certain, they would have trust in him. Also, he knows his own limits, thereby humbling himself by stating he does not know.

Certainly, this is from the completeness of *eemaan* in Allaah and fear of Him, that he does not put himself forward before his Lord and does not say about Him nor His Religion that which he does not know.

The Messenger of Allaah (*sal-Allaahu 'alayhi wa sallam*) was the most knowledgeable of all creation regarding the Religion of Allaah, and he used to be questioned regarding that which was not revealed upon him in the form of *wahee*; so he used to wait until revelation was revealed to him, then Allaah (*Subhaanahu wa Ta'aala*) would reply regarding that which His Messenger was questioned about:

3

يَسْـَٔلُونَكَ مَاذَآ أُحِلَّ لَهُمْ قُلْ أُحِلَّ لَكُمُ ٱلطَّيِّبَٰتُ

***They ask you what is lawful for them. Say: "Lawful unto you are at-Tayyibaat (all Halaal foods)."*[9]**

And He (*Subhaanahu wa Ta'aala*) says:

وَيَسْـَٔلُونَكَ

عَن ذِى ٱلْقَرْنَيْنِ قُلْ سَأَتْلُواْ عَلَيْكُم مِّنْهُ ذِكْرًا

***And they ask you about Dhul-Qarnayn. Say: "I shall recite to you something of his story."*[10]**

---

9 The Noble *Qur.aan* - *Soorah* al-Maa.idah, *Aayah* 4.

10 The Noble *Qur.aan* - *Soorah* al-Maa.idah, *Aayah* 4.

And He (*Subhaanahu wa Ta'aala*) says:

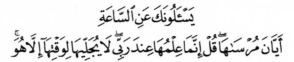

***They ask you about the Hour: "When will be its ap-
pointed time?" Say: "The knowledge thereof is with
my Lord. None can reveal its time but He."***[11]

It used to be that the *Sahaabah*, when presented with an issue about
which they did not know the Judgement of Allaah, they used to be afraid,
and chose to abstain from passing their own judgement.

So we have Abu Bakar as-Siddeeq (*radhi-yAllaahu 'anhu*) who said:
*"Which sky will shade me? And which land will harbour me if I were to
speak about the Book of Allaah without sound knowledge?"*

And we have 'Umar ibn al-Khattaab (*radhi-yAllaahu 'anhu*), when an
incident occurred, he gathered together the *Sahaabah* and began con-
sulting them regarding it.

Ibn Seereen said: *"There was none more afraid regarding that which
he did not know than Abu Bakar, and there was none after Abu Bakar
more afraid regarding that which he did not know than 'Umar ibn
al-Khattaab."*

Ibn Mas'ood (*radhi-yAllaahu 'anhu*) said: "O people! Anyone who is
questioned about that which he has knowledge of then let him speak,
and anyone who does not have knowledge then he should say, "Allaah

---

11 The Noble *Qur.aan* - *Soorah* al-A'raaf, *Aayah* 187.

knows best," for certainly from having knowledge is to say, *"Allaah knows best" regarding that which you do not know."*

Ash-Sha'bee was questioned about an issue and he said: *"I am not well-versed in it."*

So his companions said to him: *"We have become shy for you."*

So he said: *"But the angels did not become shy when it was said:*

لَا عِلْمَ لَنَآ إِلَّا مَا عَلَّمْتَنَآ

We have no knowledge except what you have taught us."[12]

And there are many examples of passing religious verdicts without sound knowledge, and amongst them are:

If a sick person's clothing became impure and it was not possible for him to purify it, then a religious verdict is passed that he should not offer his prayers until he purifies his clothing. And this religious verdict is a lie and an error. Rather, if he is unable to purify them, the sick person should offer his prayers despite his clothing and body being impure, because Allaah (*Subhaanahu wa Ta'aala*) says:

فَٱتَّقُوا۟ ٱللَّهَ مَا ٱسْتَطَعْتُمْ

So keep your duty to Allaah and fear Him as much as you can.[13]

---

12 The Noble *Qur.aan - Soorah* al-Baqarah, *Aayah* 32.

13 The Noble *Qur.aan - Soorah* at-Taghaabun, *Aayah* 16.

So the sick person offers his prayers according to his condition and his ability to do so. He prays standing, and if he is unable to do so, then sitting, and if he is unable to do so, then upon his side (lying down), nodding with his head if he is able to do so. If he is unable to do so, then some of the people of knowledge permit the blinking of the eyes, and if he is unable to blink with his eyes, and if he is sane, then he should make the intention for the act in his heart and must make the statement with his tongue.

For example, he says: *Allaahu-Akbar*, then he recites *Soorah* al-Faatihah and another *Soorah*. Then he says: *Allaahu-Akbar*, and makes the intention he is bowing down. Then he says: *Sami'a Allaahu li-man Hami-dahu*, then he makes the intention he has risen from the bowing down position. Then he says likewise in the prostration and the rest of the acts of the prayer. He makes the intention for that act which he is unable to do, so he makes the intention in his heart, and he should not delay the prayer from its time.

Because of the grave error in the aforementioned religious verdict, some Muslims die while not having prayed! And if they knew that a sick person can pray in any condition, they would have died having prayed!

Just like this issue, and many which are similar to it, it is obligatory upon the general Muslims to take religious verdicts from the people of knowledge. By this, they will know the Judgement of Allaah (*Subhaanahu wa Ta'aala*), and they will not say regarding the Religion of Allaah that which they do not know.

3. Pride

The Prophet (*sal-Allaahu 'alayhi wa sallam*) has explained this in a most clear and complete explanation, as he (*sal-Allaahu 'alayhi wa sal-*

lam) said:

Pride is ridiculing the truth (out of self-conceit) and contempt for the people. [14]

To be arrogant about the truth is to reject the truth, and to deny the people their right is to be in contempt of them. From pride and arrogance is refuting your teacher and being rude and ill-mannered towards him. Also, abstaining from one from whom benefit can be sought is from pride and arrogance.

Sadly, this befalls some of the students of knowledge. If someone informs them of something they do not have knowledge of, they abstain from it and do not accept it. Negligence of an action about which one has knowledge is an announcement of refusal and denial. We ask Allaah to improve our affairs.

Regarding this, it has been said:

العِلْمُ حَرْبٌ لِلْفَتَى الــمُتَعَالِي   كَالسَيْلِ حَرْبٌ لِلْمَكَانِ العَالِي

And the meaning of the verse: It is not possible for the proud youth to gain knowledge because knowledge is not sought with pride. So his pride is his enemy; just like the flood (of water) is unable to overcome high ground, thereby not allowing the water to settle upon it. Similarly, knowledge does not settle with pride and haughtiness, quite possibly one is deprived of knowledge because of this very reason.

---

14 *Saheeh* Muslim - The Book of *Eemaan*.

4. Being Partial to a Particular *Madhhab* and Opinion

It is obligatory for the student of knowledge to abandon the following:

Sectarianism and *hizbiyyah*, such that you join allegiance, and keep clear of something according to a particular sect or party. This, without a doubt, is contrary to the methodology of the *Salaf*. The *Salaf* were not parties, rather they were <u>one</u> party, adhering to the saying of Allaah (*Subhaanahu wa Ta'aala*):

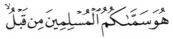

It is He Who has named you Muslims before.[15]

So there is no *hizbiyyah*, diversity, loyalty, or hostility, only according to that which is mentioned in the *Qur.aan* and the *Sunnah*. For example, from amongst the people there are those who seek *hizbiyyah* of particular groups and establish their methodology based upon evidence which can either be proof against them or proof for them. They misguide those who are upon other than their way, even though they were closer to the truth than them. They adopt a principle: *"Anyone who is not with me, then he is against me."* This is a repulsive principle, because there is a mid-point between being for you or against you, and if he is against you in truth, then he is in actual fact with you, because the Prophet (*sal-Allaahu 'alayhi wa sallam*) said:

Help your brother whether he is an oppressor or the oppressed.[16]

---

15 The Noble *Qur.aan* - *Soorah* al-Hajj, *Aayah* 78.

16 *Saheeh* al-Bukhaaree - The Book of Mathaalim (oppressions); *Saheeh* Muslim - The Book of Kindness and Family Ties.

Assisting the oppressor is to prevent him from causing oppression.

Therefore, when *hizbiyyah* began appearing amongst the Muslims and the paths became diversified and the *Ummah* became divided, some of them began misguiding the others and began "eating the flesh of their dead brother" as they were afflicted by failure, as Allaah (*Subhaanahu wa Ta'aala*) says:

And do not dispute lest you lose courage and your strength depart.[17]

Due to this, we find some students of knowledge study with a particular *Shaykh*. They stand by their *Shaykh* in truth and falsehood and show hostility to other than him, considering them to be misguided and innovators. They consider their *Shaykh* a scholar of reform and anyone other than him to be either ignorant or corrupt. And this is a great mistake; instead it is obligatory to take from whoever's speech conforms to the *Qur.aan* and the *Sunnah* and the sayings of the *Sahaabah* of the Messenger of Allaah (*sal-Allaahu 'alayhi wa sallam*).

5. Putting Oneself Forward Before Being Suitably Qualified

From that which is obligatory for precaution to be taken against, is the student of knowledge putting himself forward before being suitably qualified; for if he was to do so, then this would indicate the following:

<u>Firstly</u>: His having a high opinion of himself; that he has put himself forward, thus regarding himself as something of an authority amongst

---

17 The Noble *Qur.aan* - *Soorah* al-Anfaal, *Aayah* 46.

the distinguished;

<u>Secondly</u>: This would be indicative of his lack of understanding and knowledge of issues. Because if he has put himself forward, it is possible he has fallen into something which is not possible for him to be free of, therefore when the people see such a person, they refute him in issues so as to highlight his faults;

<u>Thirdly</u>: Certainly, if he has put himself forward before being suitably qualified, then it is certain he is speaking about the *Qur.aan* and the *Sunnah* that which he does not know. In most cases, he whose intention is this does not care and therefore responds to all he is questioned about and as a result he is hazardous with his speech at the expense of the *Qur. aan* and the *Sunnah*.

<u>Fourthly</u>: Certainly, if a person has put himself forward, then in most cases he does not accept the truth. Because in his foolishness, he assumes that if he were to succumb to other than him, even though they were upon the truth, this would be evidence that he is not a scholar.

6. Evil Suspicion

It is obligatory upon the student of knowledge to take precaution against evil suspicion about another. For example his saying, *"He does not give in charity except to show-off."* Or, *"The student does not pose this question except seeking to show-off, so that it is known he is a student with understanding."*

It was the habit of the *munaafiqoon*, that when an almsgiver came forward to offer a large amount of charity, they would say: *"Hypocrite!"* and if he was to offer a small amount of charity, they would say: *"Allaah is not in need of this charity,"* and Allaah (*Subhaanahu wa Ta'aala*) has said regarding them:

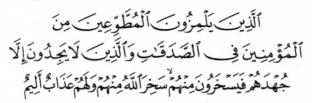

Those who defame such of the believers who give charity voluntarily, and those who could not find to give charity except what is available to them, so they mock at them, Allaah will throw back their mockery on them, and they shall have a painful torment.[18]

So be careful of falling into evil suspicion about someone who appears upright. There is no difference in having evil suspicion about your teacher or your friend, since that which is obligatory is to offer a kind thought to one who is evidently upright. As for he who is evidently not upright, then there is no harm in having evil suspicion about him in your heart. However, it is upon you to confirm this until this false impression is removed from your heart. This is because some people often have evil suspicion about someone based upon a false impression which has no basis.

So if you have evil suspicion about someone regardless of whether it is a student of knowledge or not, then it is obligatory upon you to verify whether there is clear evidence which permits you to harbour such evil suspicion. If there is, then there is no harm in this. However, if it is a totally false impression, then this is not permissible towards a Muslim whose uprightness is evident, since Allaah (*Subhaanahu wa Ta'aala*)

---

18 The Noble *Qur.aan - Soorah* at-Tawbah, *Aayah* 79.

says:

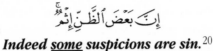

O you who believe! Avoid much suspicions.[19]

Allaah (*Subhaanahu wa Ta'aala*) did not say all suspicion, because some suspicion has a basis and is acceptable:

إِنَّ بَعْضَ ٱلظَّنِّ إِثْمٌ

Indeed <u>some</u> suspicions are sin.[20]

As for suspicion which causes hostility towards someone, then there is no doubt it is a sin. The same is the case for suspicion which has no basis. However if there is a basis, then there is no harm for you to have evil suspicion.

It is imperative for the person to assume a level that befits him, and not compromise it with corruption and evil. Rather, he should be wary of these mistakes which have been mentioned. This is because the student of knowledge has had honour conferred upon him by Allaah through knowledge, and has thus made him a model and example, such that Allaah has commanded the turning of the affairs of the people in matters of difficulty to the scholars, as He (*Subhaanahu wa Ta'aala*) says:

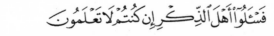

So ask the Ahl adh-Dhikr (people of the knowledge)

---

19 The Noble *Qur.aan* - *Soorah* al-Hujuraat, *Aayah* 12.

20 The Noble *Qur.aan* - *Soorah* al-Hujuraat, *Aayah* 12.

if you do not know.[21]

And He (*Subhaanahu wa Ta'aala*) says:

وَإِذَا جَآءَهُمْ أَمْرٌ مِّنَ ٱلْأَمْنِ
أَوِ ٱلْخَوْفِ أَذَاعُوا بِهِۦ وَلَوْ رَدُّوهُ إِلَى ٱلرَّسُولِ وَإِلَىٰٓ أُوْلِى
ٱلْأَمْرِ مِنْهُمْ لَعَلِمَهُ ٱلَّذِينَ يَسْتَنۢبِطُونَهُۥ مِنْهُمْ

**When there comes to them some matter touching
safety or fear, they make it known, if only they had
referred it to the Messenger or to those charged
with authority among them, the proper investiga-
tors would have understood it from them.**[22]

So that which is evident O student of knowledge, is that you are respected. Therefore, do not lower yourself to a demeaning level; rather
be like that which is befitting for you to be.

---

21 The Noble *Qur.aan* - *Soorah* al-Anbiyaa., *Aayah* 7.

22 The Noble *Qur.aan* - *Soorah* an-Nisaa., *Aayah* 83.

Chapter Four

Recommended Books for Students of Knowledge
and Islaamic Rulings related to Seeking Knowledge
and Points of Benefit.

Within this chapter there are three parts:

Part One
Recommended Books for Students of Knowledge

Part Two
Islaamic Rulings related to Seeking Knowledge

Part Three
Points of Benefit

Part One

Recommended Books for Students of Knowledge

Before beginning this chapter, it is imperative to point out some important issues for the student of knowledge, and these are:

1. How to conduct yourself with a book

Firstly - Knowing its subject: It is imperative to know the subject of the book so that you can derive benefit from it.

Secondly - Knowing its technical terminology: Knowing the terminology will assist you in saving a lot of time. This is what the scholars do in the introduction of their books. For example, we know if the author of «بُلُوْغُ الــمَرَام» was to say «مُتَّفَقٌ عَلَيْه» he means that which is agreed upon in authenticity by *Imaam* al-Bukhaaree and *Imaam* Muslim. However, the author of «الـمُنْتَقَى» differs in this matter; so if he says «مُتَّفَقٌ عَلَيْه» he means that which is agreed upon in authenticity by *Imaam* Ahmad, *Imaam* al-Bukhaaree and *Imaam* Muslim.

The same is the case with the books of *fiqh* where they differentiate between «القَوْلاَن», «الوَجْهَان», «الرّوَايَتَان» and «الاِحْتِمَالاَن».

As for «الرّوَايَتَان», then this is according to *Imaam* Ahmad, and «الوَجْهَان» is according to the major scholars from his adherents, and «الاِحْتِمَالاَن» wavers between «القَوْلاَن», and «القَوْلاَن» is more general than all of these.

Like this, he needs to know for example if the author says «إِجْمَاعاً» or «وِفَاقاً». So if he said «إِجْمَاعاً» he means amongst the *Ummah*, and if he said «وِفَاقاً» he means amongst the three *Imaams*, as is the terminology used by the author of «الفُرُوْع»; a book dealing with the *fiqh* of the Hanbalee *madhhab*. Similarly, the rest of the authors of the other *madhaahib*; each one has his own terminology, so it is imperative to know the terminology of the author.

<u>Thirdly - Knowing its style and expressions</u>: You find if you were to read a book for the first time, especially if it is a book of Islaamic knowledge, it may offer you expressions which require you to carefully consider and think about each meaning. So if you were to read the book a few times, you would understand it sufficiently, such that it would be as if you had written it.

There is a matter which is external to the issue of your conduct with a book and that is making beneficial notes in it, either in the margins or in the footnotes. It is important the student of knowledge takes advantage of the opportunity to do this. If you come across an issue that requires explanation, evidence or justification, and you fear you may forget it, then you must make a note of it either in the margin, which is either on the right or the left of the page or in the footnote, which is at the bottom of the page.

There is much which slips by a person, such as these points of benefit. However, if you were to have made a note of it, it would not have taken a minute to do, and then if you were to refer to it at a later time, it would remind you. So it is imperative for the student of knowledge to pay attention to this, especially with the books of *fiqh*. You may pass by an issue in some books which mention its ruling; however, you then may come to a standstill because of a problem. If you were to refer to the books which are broader in scope than this particular book which is before you, you will find a statement which makes the issue clearer. You should then make a note of this statement as you may wish to refer to it at another time if necessary, without having to refer to the original book from which you had taken note. You will find this is something that will save you much time.

2. Reading books is of two types

<u>Firstly - Planned and comprehensive reading</u>. It is imperative for the person to contemplate and be patient over what he reads.

<u>Secondly - Browsing and reading the book with speed</u>. This does not in itself attain comprehensive and planned reading as it did in the first type.

The ideal way to read a book is to think and reflect on the meanings of the words and to seek assistance from those who understand from the people of knowledge. No doubt, in this regard, the most deserving of books is the Book of Allaah. So you must be patient and persevere, since no-one has been given anything as good and encompassing as patience.

3. Collecting books

It is befitting for the student of knowledge to adhere to collecting books. However, you must begin with the important then move along in order of importance. If you are not in a financial position to do so, then it is neither good nor wise to buy many books which will force you at some stage to forfeit their value. This is ill-minded purchasing. If you cannot afford to buy books, then it is possible for you to borrow from any library.

4. Adhering to the important books

It is obligatory upon the student of knowledge to adhere more to the major books of the past, instead of those written recently. This is because some authors of today do not possess firm and well-rooted knowledge. As a result, if you read that which they write you will find it is shallow and superficial. They may transmit something in their own words distorting it into a long expression and rendering it absolute rubbish! So it is upon you to adhere to the major books of the *Salaf*, for certainly they are better and more blessed by far than the books of the successors.

In most cases the books of the later modern authors have little meaning and much wording and expression; you read a complete page and it is possible for you to summarise it in a line or two! However, with the books of the *Salaf* you will find them effortless to read, resilient, easy and satisfying. You will not find one word except that it has a purpose and meaning.

Amongst the most highly regarded and important books which are obligatory upon the student of knowledge to adhere to are the books of *Shaykh* al-Islaam Ibn Taymiyyah and his student Ibn al-Qayyim (*rahimahumAllaah*).

From that which is known is that the books of Ibn al-Qayyim are much easier to read and understand whilst those of *Shaykh* al-Islaam Ibn Taymiyyah are very high powered because of his more abundant knowledge and brilliance of mind. Despite being his foremost student, Ibn al-Qayyim was not a copy of Ibn Taymiyyah, rather, Ibn al-Qayyim was independent in his own right: if he saw his *Shaykh* differed with that which he felt was correct he would speak up.

Thus, he made clear his differing in opinion, and therefore he (*rahima-hullaah*) is a distinct individual of independent thought. However, there is no surprise when he agrees with his *Shaykh* (*rahima-hullaah*) in that which he saw as true and correct. Whilst there is no doubt if you carefully contemplate the general opinions of *Shaykh* al-Islaam you will find they are correct, and this is an issue that one who reflects on both their books will come to know of.

5. Categorising books

Books are divided into three categories:

First category: Good books;

Second category: Evil/corrupt books;

Third category: Books that are neither good nor evil.

So adhere to making your library free of any books which have no good in them or have evil in them. It is said that there are some books on good manners, however they waste time and bring about no benefit. And there are harmful books which have specific thoughts and a specific *manhaj*; so these books must also be excluded from your library despite them being on *manhaj* or *'aqeedah*. For example, the books of the innovators which are harmful in *'aqeedah*, and the books of rebellion and revolution which are harmful to the *manhaj*. Generally, all books that are harmful should be excluded from your library; since books are nourishment for the soul, like food and drink are for the body. If you were nourished with that which is similar to these books, then you would be afflicted with great harm, and as a result, you would pursue a path differing to the *manhaj* of the upright student of knowledge.

Recommended books for students of knowledge[1]:

Firstly – *'Aqeedah*

[1] ثلاثة الأصول   – محمد بن عبد الوهاب

[2] القواعد الأربع – محمد بن عبد الوهاب

[3] كشف الشبهات – محمد بن عبد الوهاب

[4] كتاب التوحيد – محمد بن عبد الوهاب

[5] العقيدة الواسطية – شيخ الإسلام ابن تيمية

This book [5] comprises the *Tawheed* of Allaah's *Asmaa.* and *Sifaat*, and is amongst the best that has been written in this field, and it is worthwhile reading and referring to.

[6] العقيدة الحموية – شيخ الإسلام ابن تيمية

[7] العقيدة التدمرية – شيخ الإسلام ابن تيمية

These two treatises [6] and [7] are broader than «**العقيدة الواسطية**».

---

1 Compiler's Note: Our Noble *Shaykh* was questioned regarding these books, so I noted them all here.
Translator's Note: A further list of 430 plus books recommended for students of knowledge is available in Appendix II and Appendix III.

[8] العقيدة الطحاوية – أبو جعفر حمد بن محمد الطحاوي

[9] شرح العقيدة الطحاوية – أبو الحسن علي بن أبي العز

[10] الدرر السنية في الأجوبة النجدية – عبد الرحمن بن قاسم

Secondly – Hadeeth

[1] فتح الباري شرح صحيح البخاري – الحافظ ابن حجر العسقلاني

[2] سبل السلام شرح بلوغ المرام – الصنعاني

This [2] is a comprehensive book combining both *hadeeth* and *fiqh*.

[3] نيل الأوطار شرح منتقى الأخبار – الشوكاني

[4] عمدة الأحكام – المقدسي

This [4] is a specialised book. In addition, the fact that all the *ahaadeeth* mentioned are to be found in *Saheeh* al-Bukhaaree and *Saheeh* Muslim, means there is no need to search into their authenticity.

[5] الأربعين النووية – أبو زكرية النووي

This [5] is a good book, because it mentions etiquette and its approach is also good, as well as it mentioning some very important rules, such as the saying of the Messenger of Allaah (*sal-Allaahu 'alayhi wa sallam*):

From a man's perfecting his religion is his leaving

that which does not concern him.[2]

With this particular rule, if you were to make it a path you pursued, it would be enough for you. Like this, there is the rule regarding speech found in the saying of the Messenger of Allaah (*sal-Allaahu 'alayhi wa sallam*):

Whoever believes in Allaah and the Last Day should speak good or remain quiet.[3]

[6] بلوغ المرام – الحافظ ابن حجر العسقلاني

This [6] is a most beneficial book, especially in that it mentions the narrators of the *hadeeth* and who has made a narration *saheeh* or *da'eef*, and he has also commented on the *ahaadeeth*.

[7] نخبة الفكر – الحافظ ابن حجر العسقلاني

This [7] is a comprehensive book that, if the student of knowledge were to understand well and master, would be sufficient for him and better than many books in *mustalah al-hadeeth*. Ibn Hajar has a beneficial approach in his works and that is dividing the different topics into appropriate parts and studying them thoroughly and carefully. So if the stu-

---

2 *Musnad* of *Imaam* Ahmad – Volume 1, Page 201;
at-Tirmidhee – Number 2318;
Riyaadhus-Saaliheen of an-Nawawee – Page 73, where it mentions: the *hadeeth* has been declared *hasan*;
Ahmad Shaakir has authenticated the *hadeeth* in *al-Musnad*, number 1737.

3 *Saheeh* al-Bukhaaree – The Book of Manners;
Saheeh Muslim – The Book of Gathering.

dent of knowledge were to read them, he would find it vibrant since it is based upon an active and investigative mind, and I further recommend the student of knowledge to memorise it because it is a most beneficial summary in *mustalah al-hadeeth*.

[8] الكتب الستة
- صحيح البخاري
- صحيح مسلم
- أبو داود
- الترمذي
- النسائي
- ابن ماجه

I also advise the student of knowledge to spend time reading the afore-mentioned books, since with them are two benefits:

Firstly: Referring to the principles;

Secondly: The recurrence of the names of the *rijaal* upon the mind. With this, if you were to pass by a name from amongst the narrators mentioned in *Saheeh al-Bukhaaree* in any chain, then you will come to know it to be one of his narrators, and with this the student of knowledge will benefit.

Thirdly – *Fiqh*

[1] آداب المشي إلى الصلاة – محمد بن عبد الوهاب
[2] زاد المستقنع في اختصار المقنع – الحجاوي

This [2] is one of the best texts in *fiqh* and it is a blessed and comprehensive book. Our *Shaykh*, 'Abdur-Rahmaan as-Sa'dee (*rahima-hullaah*) recommended we memorise this book, whilst he himself had memorised the text of «دليل الطالب».

[3] الروض المربع شرح زاد المستقنع – منصور البهوتي

[4] عمدة الفقه – ابن قدامة

Fourthly – *Faraa.id*

[1] متن الرحبية – الرحبي

[2] متن البرهانية – محمد البرهاني

This book [2] is a beneficial and comprehensive summary for all aspects of *faraa.id*. I find that «متن البرهانية» is better than «الرحبية» because «متن البرهانية» is more complete and comprehensive than «الرحبية».

Fifthly – *Tafseer*

[1] تفسير القرآن العظيم – ابن كثير

This book [1] is good with respect to *tafseer* and *aathaar*. However, it is not very vast in terms of *i'raab* and *balaaghah*.

[2] تيسير الكريم الرحمن في تفسير كلام المنان – عبد الرحمن السعدي

This [2] is a good, easy and reliable book and I advise it be read.

[3] المقدمة في التفسير – شيخ الإسلام ابن تيمية

This book [3] is a very important introduction to the subject of *tafseer*.

146

[4] أضواء البيان – محمد الأمين الشنقيطي

This [4] is a comprehensive book incorporating all the fields of *hadeeth*, *fiqh*, *tafseer* and *usool al-fiqh*.

6. General books on some areas

Nahoo

[1] متن الآجرومية – الصنهاجي

This [1] is a short and simple book.

[2] ألفية ابن مالك – ابن مالك

This book [2] is a summary of the rules of *nahoo*.

With respect to the life and times of the Messenger of Allaah (*sal-Allaahu 'alayhi wa sallam*):

[3] زاد المعاد – ابن القيم

This [3] is a very beneficial book. The author relates the life of the Messenger of Allaah (*sal-Allaahu 'alayhi wa sallam*) in all circumstances whereby he derives from them many rulings.

[4] روضة العقلاء – ابن حبان البستي

This [4] is a beneficial and concise book in that it incorporates many points of benefit and traditions of the scholars, the *muhaddithoon* and other than them.

[5] سير أعلام النبلاء – الذهبي

This book [5] is beneficial and it is befitting for the student of knowledge to read and refer to it.

Part Two

Religious Verdicts related to Seeking Knowledge

al-Hamdu Lillaah - these have now been translated, and the translation is being revised; *inshaa.-Allaah* they will feature in Volume 2.

Part Three

Points of Benefit and Treatises

al-Hamdu Lillaah - these have now been translated, and the translation is being revised; *inshaa.-Allaah* they will feature in Volume 3.

Appendices

Within this section there are two parts:

Appendix I
Sayings of the *Imaams* regarding following the *Sunnah*
and ignoring their views contradictory to it

Appendix II
List of over 130 books
recommended for students of knowledge

Appendix III
List of over 300 further books
recommended for students of knowledge

<u>Important Note</u>: These appendices are not attributed to the authorship of the Noble *Shaykh* Muhammad ibn Saalih al-'Uthaymeen. Rather, the translator has sourced and put together some very important material which will benefit the reader, and most importantly the sincere student of knowledge, *inshaa.-Allaah*.

Appendix I

Sayings of the *Imaam*s regarding following the *Sunnah* and ignoring their views contradictory to it

Allaah, Mighty and Sublime, says:

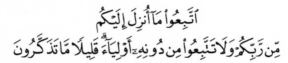

Follow (O men!) the revelation given to you from your Lord, and follow not, as friends and protectors, other than Him. Little is it you remember of admonition.[1]

1. *Imaam* Abu Haneefah (*rahima-hullaah*)[2]

The first of them is Abu Haneefah Nu'maan ibn Thaabit, whose companions have narrated from him various sayings and diverse warnings, all of them leading to one thing: the obligation to accept the *Hadeeth*, and to

---

1 For a comprehensive list of references, refer to *Shaykh* Muhammad Naasiruddeen al-Albaanee's English edition of "The Prophet's Prayer" - Introduction, Pages 7 through to 14.

2 The Noble *Qur.aan* - *Soorah* al-A'raaf, *Aayah* 3.

give up following the opinions of the *Imaams* which contradict it:

1. *"When a hadeeth is found to be saheeh, then that is my madhhab."*

2. *"It is not permitted for anyone to accept our views if they do not know from where we got them."*

In one narration, *"It is prohibited for someone who does not know my evidence to give verdicts on the basis of my words."*

Another narration adds, *"...for we are mortals: we say one thing one day, and take it back the next day."*

In another narration, *"Woe to you, O Ya'qoob! Do not write down everything you hear from me, for it happens that I hold one opinion today and reject it tomorrow, or hold one opinion tomorrow and reject it the day after tomorrow."*

3. *"When I say something contradicting the Book of Allaah the Exalted or what is narrated from the Messenger (sal-Allaahu 'alayhi wa sallam), then ignore my saying."*

2. *Imaam* Maalik ibn Anas (*rahima-hullaah*)

As for *Imaam* Maalik ibn Anas, he said:

1. *"Truly I am only a mortal: I make mistakes (sometimes) and I am correct (sometimes). Therefore, look into my opinions: all that agrees with the Book and the Sunnah, accept it; and all that does not agree with the Book and the Sunnah, ignore it."*

2. *"Everyone after the Prophet (sal-Allaahu 'alayhi wa sallam) will*

have his sayings accepted and rejected - not so the Prophet (sal-Allaahu 'alayhi wa sallam)."

3. Ibn Wahb said: *"I heard Maalik being asked about cleaning between the toes during ablution. He said, 'The people do not have to do that.' I did not approach him until the crowd had lessened, when I said to him, 'We know of a sunnah about that.' He said, 'What is that?' I said, 'Layth ibn Sa'd, Ibn Lahee'ah and 'Amr ibn al-Haarith narrated to us from Yazeed ibn 'Amr al-Ma'aafiree from Abu 'Abdur-Rahman al-Hubulee from Mustawrid ibn Shaddaad al-Qurashee who said, 'I saw the Messenger of Allaah (sal-Allaahu 'alayhi wa sallam) rubbing between his toes with his little finger.' He said, 'This hadeeth is sound; I had not heard of it at all until now.' Afterwards, I heard him being asked about the same thing, on which he ordered cleaning between the toes."*

3. Imaam ash-Shaafi'ee (rahima-hullaah)

As for *Imaam* ash-Shaafi'ee, the quotations from him are most numerous and beautiful, and his followers were the best in sticking to them:

1. *"The Sunnahs of the Messenger of Allaah (sal-Allaahu 'alayhi wa sallam) reach, as well as escape from, every one of us. So whenever I voice my opinion, or formulate a principle, where something contrary to my view exists on the authority of the Messenger of Allaah (sal-Allaahu 'alayhi wa sallam), then the correct view is what the Messenger of Allaah (sal-Allaahu 'alayhi wa sallam) has said, and it is my view."*

2. *"The Muslims are unanimously agreed that if a Sunnah of the Messenger of Allaah (sal-Allaahu 'alayhi wa sallam) is made clear to someone, it is not permitted for him to leave it for the saying of anyone else."*

3. *"If you find in my writings something different to the Sunnah of the Messenger of Allaah (sal-Allaahu 'alayhi wa sallam), then speak on the basis of the Sunnah of the Messenger of Allaah (sal-Allaahu 'alayhi wa sallam), and leave what I have said."*

In one narration: *"...then follow it (the Sunnah), and do not look sideways at anyone else's saying."*

4. *"When a hadeeth is found to be saheeh, then that is my madhhab."*

5. *"You are more knowledgeable about Hadeeth than I, so when a hadeeth is saheeh, inform me of it, whether it is from Koofah, Basrah or Syria, so that I may take the view of the hadeeth, as long as it is saheeh."*

6. *"In every issue where the people of narration find a report from the Messenger of Allaah (sal-Allaahu 'alayhi wa sallam) to be saheeh which is contrary to what I have said, then I take my saying back, whether during my life or after my death."*

7. *"If you see me saying something, and contrary to it is authentically-reported from the Prophet (sal-Allaahu 'alayhi wa sallam), then know that my intelligence has departed."*

8. *"For everything I say, if there is something authentic from the Prophet (sal-Allaahu 'alayhi wa sallam) contrary to my saying, then the hadeeth of the Prophet (sal-Allaahu 'alayhi wa sallam) comes first, so do not follow my opinion."*

9. *"Every statement on the authority of the Prophet (sal-Allaahu 'alayhi wa sallam) is also my view, even if you do not hear it from me."*

4. *Imaam* Ahmad ibn Hanbal (*rahima-hullaah*)

Imaam Ahmad was the foremost among the *Imaam*s in collecting the *Sunnah* and sticking to it, so much so that he even "disliked that a book consisting of deductions and opinions be written." Because of this he said:

1. *"Do not follow my opinion; neither follow the opinion of Maalik, nor ash-Shaafi'ee, nor Awzaa'ee, nor Thawree, but take from where they took."*

In one narration: *"Do not copy your Deen from anyone of these, but whatever comes from the Prophet (sal-Allaahu 'alayhi wa sallam) and his companions, take it; next are their Successors, where a man has a choice."*

Once he said: *"Following means that a man follows what comes from the Prophet (sal-Allaahu 'alayhi wa sallam) and his companions; after the Successors, he has a choice."*

2. *"The opinion of Awzaa'ee, the opinion of Maalik, the opinion of Abu Haneefah: all of it is opinion, and it is all equal in my eyes. However, the proof is in the narrations (from the Prophet (sal-Allaahu 'alayhi wa sallam) and his companions)."*

3. *"Whoever rejects a statement of the Messenger of Allaah (sal-Allaahu 'alayhi wa sallam) is on the brink of destruction."*

These are the clear, lucid sayings of the *Imaam*s (*rahima-humullaah*) about sticking to the *Hadeeth* and forbidding the following of their opinion without clearly-visible evidence, such that mere opinion and interpretation is not acceptable.

Hence, whoever adhered to whatever of the *Sunnah* that was proved authentic, even if it opposed some of the *Imaams'* sayings, he would not be conflicting with their *madhhab*, nor straying from their path; rather, such a person would be following all of them and would be grasping the most trustworthy hand-hold, which never breaks. However, this would not be the case with the one who abandoned any of the authentic *Sunnah* simply because it contradicted their views; nay, such a person would be being disobedient to them and opposing their above mentioned sayings, while Allaah says:

فَلَا وَرَبِّكَ لَا يُؤْمِنُونَ

حَتَّىٰ يُحَكِّمُوكَ فِيمَا شَجَرَ بَيْنَهُمْ ثُمَّ لَا يَجِدُواْ

فِى أَنفُسِهِمْ حَرَجًا مِّمَّا قَضَيْتَ وَيُسَلِّمُواْ تَسْلِيمًا

But no, by Your Lord, they can have no (real) faith, until they make you judge in all disputes between them, and find in their souls no resistance against your decisions, but accept them with the fullest conviction.[3]

He also says:

فَلْيَحْذَرِ الَّذِينَ يُخَالِفُونَ عَنْ أَمْرِهِۦٓ

أَن تُصِيبَهُمْ فِتْنَةٌ أَوْ يُصِيبَهُمْ عَذَابٌ أَلِيمٌ

Then let those beware who withstand the Messenger's order, lest some trial befall them or a grievous penalty be inflicted on them.[4]

---

3 The Noble *Qur.aan* - *Soorah* an-Nisaa., *Aayah* 65.

4 The Noble *Qur.aan* - *Soorah* an-Noor, *Aayah* 63.

al-Haafiz Ibn Rajab al-Hanbalee (*rahima-hullaah*) says:

"Therefore it is obligatory on anyone who hears of a command of the Messenger of Allaah (sal-Allaahu 'alayhi wa sallam) or knows it, to explain it to the Ummah, advise them sincerely, and order them to follow his command, even if it contradicts the opinion of someone great. This is because the authority of the Messenger of Allaah (sal-Allaahu 'alayhi wa sallam) has the most right to be respected and followed, over and above the opinion of anyone great who has unknowingly contradicted the Messenger's command in any matter. This is why the companions and those after would refute anyone who contradicted the authentic Sunnah, sometimes being very stern in their refutation, not out of hatred for that person, for they loved and respected him, but because the Messenger of Allaah was more beloved to them, and his command was superior to the command of any other created being. Hence, when the order of the Messenger and that of someone else conflicted, the order of the Messenger would be more fitting to be enforced and followed.

None of this would stop them respecting the person they had opposed because they knew that he would be forgiven; in fact, the latter would not mind his instruction being opposed when the command of the Messenger of Allaah (sal-Allaahu 'alayhi wa sallam) was clearly shown to be opposite."

Indeed, how could they mind that, when they had ordered their followers to do so, as we have seen, and had enjoined on them to abandon any of their views which contradicted the *Sunnah*. In fact, *Imaam* ash-Shaafi'ee (*rahima-hullaah*) told his companions to attribute the authentic *Sunnah* to him also, even if he had not adopted it or had adopted something contradictory to it. Hence, when the analyst Ibn Daqeeq al-'Eed (*rahima-hullaah*) collected together, in a bulky volume, the issues in which one or more of the four *Imaams'* *madhhab*s had contradicted the authentic *hadeeth*, he wrote at the beginning of it, *"It is prohibited* *to attribute these answers to the Mujtahid Imaams, and obligatory on the jurists who follow their opinions to know of these so that they do not quote them regarding these and thus lie against them."*

To sum up: I sincerely hope that no follower of an *Imaam* will race to condemn the principles of this book and abandon benefiting from the sunnahs of the Prophet (*sal-Allaahu 'alayhi wa sallam*) which it contains, with the argument that they are contrary to his *Madhhab*. I hope that such a person will instead consider what we have given of the exhortations of the *Imaam*s towards the obligation to act on the *Sunnah* and ignore their sayings contradictory to it. I hope also that he will realise that to condemn the attitude of this book is to condemn whichever *Imaam* he is following, for we have taken these principles from those *Imaam*s, as we have explained. Therefore, whoever refuses to be guided by them on this path is in great danger, for such refusal necessitates turning away from the *Sunnah*, the *Sunnah* to which we have been ordered to refer in cases of difference of opinion and on which we have been commanded to depend.

I ask Allaah to make us among those about whom He says:

إِنَّمَا كَانَ قَوْلَ ٱلْمُؤْمِنِينَ إِذَا دُعُوٓاْ إِلَى ٱللَّهِ وَرَسُولِهِۦ لِيَحْكُمَ بَيْنَهُمْ أَن يَقُولُواْ سَمِعْنَا وَأَطَعْنَا وَأُوْلَٰٓئِكَ هُمُ ٱلْمُفْلِحُونَ ۝ وَمَن يُطِعِ ٱللَّهَ وَرَسُولَهُۥ وَيَخْشَ ٱللَّهَ وَيَتَّقْهِ فَأُوْلَٰٓئِكَ هُمُ ٱلْفَآئِزُونَ

The answer of the believers, when summoned to Allaah and His Messenger, in order that he may judge between them, is no other than this: they say, "We hear and we obey" - it is such as these that will attain Success. It is those who obey Allaah and His Messenger, and fear Allaah, and keep their duty to

Him, who will triumph.[5]

---

5 The Noble *Qur.aan* - *Soorah* an-Noor, *Aayah*s 51-52.

Appendix II

List of over 130 books
recommended for students of knowledge

In addition to the books *Shaykh* Ibn 'Uthaymeen mentioned in Chapter Four, the following comprises a list of over 130 further books recommended for students of knowledge. The list is divided into three separate stages, incorporating: beginner, intermediate and advanced; including their respective subjects:

1. Stage One – Beginner

العقيدة الإسلامية

عقيدة السلف أصحاب الحديث – أبو عثمان الصابوني	☐
الثلاثة أصول و أدلتها – محمد بن عبد الوهاب	☐
شرح العقيدة الواسطية – محمد خليل هراس	☐

القرآن الكريم

القرآن الكريم	☐
حق التلاوة – حسني شيخ عثمان	☐
الإنفاق في علوم القرآن – السيوطي	☐

التفسير

مقدمة في أصول التفسير – شيخ الإسلام ابن تيمية

تيسير الكريم الرحمن في تفسير كلام المنان – عبد الرحمن السعدي

تفسير آيات الأحكام – مناع القطان

الحديث النبوي

الأربعون النووية – الإمام النووي

رياض الصالحين – الإمام النووي

جامع العلوم و الحكم – ابن رجب

تيسير العلام شرح عمدة الأحكام – عبد الله بن عبد الرحمن البسام

توضيح الأحكام من بلوغ المرام – عبد الله بن عبد الرحمن البسام

مصطلح الحديث

نزهة النظر شرح نخبة الفكر – ابن حجر

تيسير مصطلح الحديث – محمود الطحان

تيسير علوم الحديث للمبتدئين – عمرو عبد المنعم سليم

كتب التخريج

الدراية – ابن حجر

الصحابة و رجال الحديث

منيف الرتبة لمن ثبت له شريف الصحبة – العلائي

إجمال الإصابة – العلائي

المعاجم الحديثية

المقاصد الحسنة – السخاوي

دفاع عن السنة

منزلة السنة في الإسلام – محمد ناصر الدين الألباني

السنة في التشريع الإسلامي – محمد أمان الجامي

الأخلاق و السلوك

الأخلاق و السير في مداواة النفوس – الإمام ابن حزم الأندلسي

الإخلاص – حسين العوايشة

الفقه

فقه السنة – سيد سابق

الروضة الندية – صديق حسن خان

أصول الفقه

هدية السلطان إلى مسلمي بلاد اليابان – محمد سلطان المعصومي

الواضح في أصول الفقه للمبتدئين – محمد سليمان عبد الله الأشقر

القواعد الفقهية و نظريات الفقه

القواعد – ابن رجب

II

البدع

البدعة و أثرها السيء في الأمة – سليم الهلالي

السنن و المبتدعات – محمد عبد السلام الشقيري

163

السلوك و الإحسان

الأذكار – النووي ☐

رياض الصالحين – النووي ☐

الـملل و الفرق

تلبيس إبليس – ابن الجوزي ☐

التاريخ

التاريخ الإسلامي – محمود شاكر الحرستاني ☐

الإمامة و السياسة – ابن قتيبة ☐

النحو و الصرف

ملخص قواعد اللغة العربية – فؤاد نعمة ☐

النحو الواضح – علي الجازم و مصطفى أمين ☐

توضيح النحو شرح ابن عقيل – عبد العزيز محمد فاخر ☐

توضيح الصرف – عبد العزيز محمد فاخر ☐

مفردات اللغة

مختار الصحاح – محمد بن أبي بكر الرازي ☐

البلاغة

البلاغة الواضحة – علي الجازم و مصطفى أمين ☐

معاجم اللغة

المصباح المنير – الفيومي ☐

164

2. Stage Two – Intermediate

العقيدة الإسلامية

فتح المجيد شرح كتاب التوحيد – عبد الرحمن بن حسن

القرآن الكريم

الصحيح المسند من أسباب النزول – مقبل بن هادي الوادعي

التفسير

تفسير القرآن العظيم – الإمام ابن كثير الدمشقي

الحديث النبوي

صحيح الإمام البخاري – الإمام البخاري

صحيح الإمام مسلم – الإمام مسلم

سلسلة الأحاديث الضعيفة و أثرها السيء في الأمة – الألباني

سبل السلام – الصنعاني

بهجة النفوس شرح مختصر البخاري – ابن أبي جمرة

مصطلح الحديث

الباعث الحثيث – أحمد شاكر

الحطة في ذكر الصحاح الستة – صديق حسن خان

فتح المغيث شرح ألفية الحديث – العراقي

الصحابة و رجال الحديث

الإصابة في تمييز الصحابة – ابن حجر

تقريب التهذيب – ابن حجر

الـمعاجم الحديثية

إرواء الغليل في تخريج أحاديث منار السبيل – الألباني

دفاع عن السنة

مفتاح الجنة في الاحتجاج بالسنة – الإمام السيوطي

الأخلاق و السلوك

الفوائد – ابن قيم الجوزية

الوابل الصيب – ابن قيم الجوزية

مختصر منهاج القاصدين – ابن قدامة المقدسي

الفقه

المغني – ابن قدامة

المحلى – ابن حزم الأندلسي

أصول الفقه

الرسالة – الإمام الشافعي

القواعد الفقهية و نظريات الفقه

الأشباه و النظائر – ابن نجيم و السيوطي

البدع

الحوادث و البدع – الطرطوشي

السلوك و الإحسان

مختصر منهاج القاصدين – ابن قدامة

الملل و الفرق

الفرق بين الفرق – عبد القاهر البغدادي

الملل و النحل – الشهرستاني

أسرار الأحكام

حجة الله البالغة – الدهلوي

السيرة

السيرة النبوية – الإمام الذهبي

الروض الأنف شرح سيرة ابن هشام – سهيلي

التاريخ

الشماريخ في علم التاريخ – الإمام السيوطي

دول الإسلام – الإمام الذهبي

الكامل – ابن الأثير

النحو و الصرف

الموجز في قواعد اللغة العربية – سعيد الأفغاني

شرح الألفية – ابن عقيل

II

مفردات اللغة

المعجم الوسيط – مجمع اللغة العربية ☐

البلاغة

علوم البلاغة – أحمد مصطفى المراغي ☐

الإيضاح – التلخيص ☐

المفتاح – القزويني ☐

الأدب

أدب الكاتب – ابن قتيبة ☐

معاجم اللغة

القاموس المحيط – الفيروزآبادي ☐

3. Stage Three – Advanced

العقيدة الإسلامية

شرح العقيدة الطحاوية – ابن أبي العز الحنفي ☐

مختصر العلو للعلي الغفار – الإمام الذهبي / الألباني ☐

مختصر الصواعق المرسلة على الجهمية و المعطلة – ابن قيم الجوزية ☐

الرسالة التدمرية – ابن تيمية ☐

الفتوى الحموية – ابن تيمية ☐

القرآن الكريم

البرهان في علوم القرآن – الزركشي

حجة القراءات – ابن زنجلة

علوم القرآن – الزركشي

التفسير

جامع البيان في تفسير القرآن – ابن جرير الطبري

الجامع لأحكام القرآن – القرطبي

أحكام القرآن – ابن العربي

أحكام القرآن – الجصاص

الحديث النبوي

جامع الأصول من أحاديث الرسول – ابن الأثير

فتح الباري في شرح صحيح البخاري – ابن حجر العسقلاني

جامع الأصول – ابن الأثير

مصطلح الحديث

أصول التخريج و دراسة الأسانيد – محمود الطحان

دراسات في الحديث النبوي – محمد مصطفى الأعظمي

فتح المغيث في شرح ألفية الحديث – السخاوي

التأصيل لعلم التخريج و قواعد الجرح و التعديل – بكر أبو زيد

تدريب الراوي – السيوطي

التهذيب – ابن حجر

II

169

الـمعاجم الحديثية

المعجم المفهرس لألفاظ الحديث النبوي

الأخلاق و السلوك

مدارج السالكين – ابن قيم الجوزية

الفقه

نيل الأوطار – الشوكاني

الموسوعة الفقهية – الكويتية

أصول الفقه

الموافقات – أبو إسحاق الشاطبي

الإحكام في أصول الأحكام – ابن حزم الأندلسي

إرشاد الفحول – الشوكاني

البحر المحيط – الزركشي

فقه الدعوة

منهج الأنبياء في الدعوة إلى الله – ربيع بن هادي المدخلي

طريق الدعوة إلى الإسلام – محمد أمان الجامي

البدع

الاعتصام – أيو إسحاق الشاطبي

السلوك و الإحسان

مختصر منهاج القاصدين – ابن قدامة

170

الـملل والفرق

منهاج السنة النبوية – ابن تيمية

الفتاوى

الفتاوى الكبرى – ابن تيمية

أسرار الأحكام

الموافقات – الشاطبي

السلوك والإحسان

مفتاح دار السعادة – ابن القيم

مدارج السالكين – ابن القيم

السيرة

الروض الأنف – السهيلي

زاد المعاد – ابن القيم

التاريخ

البداية والنهاية – ابن كثير

النحو والصرف

جامع الدروس العربية – مصطفى الغلاييني

II

البلاغة

أسرار البلاغة ودلائل الإعجاز – عبد القاهر الجرجاني

دلائل الإعجاز – عبد القاهر الجرجاني

171

الأدب

تاريخ آداب العرب – مصطفى صادق الرافعي

معاجم اللغة

لسان العرب – ابن منظور

This list is by no means exhaustive, rather, it is merely a good starting point for the student of knowledge who embarks upon building his very own personal library, *inshaa.-Allaah*!

Appendix III

List of over 300 further books recommended for students of knowledge

For those who are well on their way to building their own personal library, the following list of over 300 books will provide a more comprehensive listing, *inshaa.-Allaah*.

تفسير القرآن

	تفسير ابن جرير الطبري
	تفسير ابن أبي حاتم / بتحقيق دار الباز
	أضواء البيان للشنقيطي
	الدر المنثور للسيوطي
	تفسير البغوي / بتحقيق النمر و آخرون
	تفسير ابن الجوزي
	تفسير ابن كثير / بتحقيق السلامة
	تفسير ابن عطية / بتحقيق جمع من المغاربة
	تفسير الجلالين / بتحقيق أحمد شاكر و أخوه
	تفسير الآلوسي / بتحقيق محمد العرب

تفسير ابن سعدي / بتحقيق اللويحق ☐
تفسير الشوكاني / بتحقيق أحمد السيد و آخرون ☐

أحكام القرآن
تفسير ابن العربي / بتحقيق علي البجاوي ☐
تفسير القرطبي / بتحقيق محمود بن عثمان ☐

تناسب القرآن
تفسير البقاعي / الطبعة الهندية ☐

إعراب القرآن
الدر النضيد للسمين / أحسن منها طبعة الخراط لكنها لم تكتمل ☐
الإعراب المفصل لدرويش / الطبعة الأخيرة ☐

فضائل القرآن
فضائل القرآن لابن كثير / بتحقيق أبو إسحاق الحويني ☐
موسوعة فضائل القرآن للطرهوني ☐

أسباب النزول
أسباب النزول للواحدي / بتحقيق عصام الحميدان ☐
العجاب لابن حجر / بتحقيق عبد الحكيم الأنيس – غير كامل ☐
لباب النقول للسيوطي ☐

أصول التفسير و قواعده
مقدمة في أصول التفسير لابن تيمية / بتحقيق فؤاد زمرلي ☐

قواعد التفسير الترجيحية لحسين الحربي ☐

قواعد التفسير للسبت ☐

ألفاظ القرآن

مفردات ألفاظ القرآن للراغب / بتحقيق الداوودي ☐

أنواع علوم القرآن

البرهان في علوم القرآن للزركشي ☐

الإتقان للسيوطي ☐

مناهل العرفان للزرقاني ☐

القراءات

القراءات و أثرها لعمر بازمول ☐

إعراب القراءات السبع و عللها لابن خالويه / بتحقيق العثيمين ☐

الوافي في شرح الشاطبية للقاضي ☐

المفسرون

التفسير و المفسرون لحسين الذهبي ☐

اتجاهات التفسير في القرن الرابع لفهد الرومي ☐

التجويد

فتح المجيد في حكم القراءة بالتجويد لسعود ☐

سنن القاء للقارئ ☐

شرح تحفة الأطفال للضباع / بتحقيق أشرف عبد المقصود ☐

III

175

شرح منظومة ابن الجزري لملا علي القارئ / الطبعة المحققة	
التمهيد في علم التجويد لابن الجزري / بتحقيق البواب	

مصطلح الحديث

نزهة النظر لابن حجر / بتحقيق نور الدين عتر	
شرح الشرح لملا علي قارئ / بتحقيق ابنا نزار	
علوم الحديث لابن الصلاح / بتحقيق نور الدين عتر	
الباعث الحثيث لابن كثير / بتحقيق علي الحلبي	
فتح المغيث للسخاوي / بتحقيق علي حسين	
تدريب الراوي للسيوطي / بتحقيق نظر الفاريابي	
توضيح الأفكار للصنعاني / بتحقيق محمد محي الدين	
الموقظة للذهبي / بتحقيق أبو غدة	
توجيه النظر للجزائري / بتحقيق أبو غدة	

تاريخ مصطلح الحديث

اهتمام المحدثين بالحديث للقمان	
علم الرجال و أهميته للمعلمي / بتحقيق علي الحلبي	

قواعد مصطلح الحديث

الرفع و التكميل للكنوي / بتحقيق أبو غدة	
أربع مسائل في علوم الحديث / بتحقيق أبو غدة	
شفاء العليل لأبي الحسن مصطفى	
ضوابط الجرح و التعديل لعبد العزيز آل عبد اللطيف	

	دراسات في الجرح و التعديل للأعظمي
	المنهج الإسلامي لفاروق حمادة

الكتب المسندة

	مسند أحمد بن حنبل / بتحقيق دار إحياء التراث العربي
	صحيح البخاري / بتحقيق أحمد شاكر
	صحيح مسلم / بتحقيق محمد فؤاد عبد الباقي
	سنن أبي داود / بتحقيق محمد عوامة
	سنن الترمذي / بتحقيق أحمد شاكر
	سنن النسائي / بتحقيق المكتب الإسلامي
	سنن ابن ماجه / بتحقيق محمد فؤاد عبد الباقي / هنـاك طبعة بعناية محمد الأعظمي – أحسن و أتقن

	صحيح ابن خزيمة / بتحقيق الأعظمي
	صحيح ابن حبان / بتحقيق الأرناؤوط و بترتيب ابن بلبان
	مستدرك الحاكم / الطبعة الهندية
	موطأ مالك / بتحقيق محمد فؤاد عبد الباقي
	سنن الدارمي / بتحقيق زمرلي و آخر
	معجم الأوسط / بتحقيق طارق بن عوض الله و آخر
	المعجم الصغير للطبراني
	السنن الكبرى للبيهقي / معه الجوهر النقي و فهارس السنن
	السنن الصغرى للبيهقي / بتحقيق عبد السلام عبد الشافي
	شعب الإيمان للبيهقي / بتحقيق زغلول

III

سنن الدارقطني / له فهارس الدارقطني لمرعشلي □

مصنف ابن أبي شيبة / بتحقيق ضبط كمال الحوت □

مصنف عبد الرزاق الصنعاني / بتحقيق الأعظمي □

مسند البزار / بتحقيق محفوظ الرحمن □

سنن سعيد بن منصور / بتحقيق سعد آل حميد □

مسند أبي يعلى الموصلي / بتحقيق حسين أسد □

الأدب المفرد للبخاري / بتحقيق الألباني □

متون جامعة

جامع الأصول لابن الأثير / بتحقيق الأرناؤوط □

مجمع الزوائد للهيثمي / بتحقيق حسين أسد □

المطالب العالية لابن حجر / بتحقيق غنيم بن عباس و آخر □

بلوغ المرام لابن حجر / بتحقيق سمير الزهيري □

عمدة الأحكام للمقدسي / بتحقيق الأرناؤوط □

رياض الصالحين للنووي / بتحقيق الألباني □

الأذكار للنووي / بتحقيق سليم الهلالي □

فقه الحديث

التمهيد لابن عبد البر / بتحقيق سعيد أعراب □

الاستذكار لابن عبد البر / بتحقيق قلعة جي □

شرح السنة للبغوي / بتحقيق الأرناؤوط □

فتح الباري لابن حجر / بمراجعة ابن باز □

شرح صحيح مسلم للنووي / بتحقيق مؤسسة قرطبة	
عون المعبود / بتحقيق شمس الحق	
تحفة الأحوذي للمباركفوري / طبعة الريان	
دليل الفالحين شرح رياض الصالحين للصديقي	
الفتوحات الربانية على الأذكار النووية للصديقي	
سبل السلام للصنعاني / بتحقيق محمد صبحي حلاق	
نيل الأوطار للشوكاني / بتحقيق أحمد السيد و آخران	
فيض القدير للمناوي / الطبعة الهندية	
فضل الله الصمد للجيلاني / بتحقيق محب الدين الخطيب	

غريب الحديث والأثر

غريب الحديث للخطابي / بتحقيق عبد الكريم الفرباوي	
النهاية لابن الأثير / بتحقيق الطناحي و آخر	

الأحاديث المشتهرة على الألسنة

المقاصد الحسنة للسخاوي	
كشف الخفاء للعجلوني	

تخريج الحديث

التلخيص الحبير لابن حجر / بتحقيق أبو عصام بن قطب	
الدراية في تخريج أحاديث الهداية لابن حجر	
إرواء الغليل للألباني / صنع صالح آل الشيخ تكميلاً للإرواء سماه – التكميل لما فات صاحب إرواء الغليل	

III

179

السلسلة الصحيحة و الضعيفة للألباني ☐

الأحاديث الموضوعة

تنزيه الشريعة لابن عراق / بتحقيق عبد الوهاب و آخرون ☐

مشكل الحديث

شرح مشكل الآثار للطحاوي / بتحقيق الأرناؤوط ☐

تأويل مختلف الحديث لابن قتيبة / بتحقيق محمد عبد الرحيم ☐

كتب جامعة مسندة

شرح اعتقاد أهل السنة للالكائي / بتحقيق الغامدي ☐

الإبانة الكبرى لابن بطة / رسائل علمية ☐

الشريعة للآجري / بتحقيق الوليد الناصر؛ و طبعة أخرى للدميجي ☐

عقيدة السلف لأبي عثمان الصابوني / بتحقيق ناصر الجديع ☐

السنة لابن أبي عاصم / بتحقيق الجوابرة ☐

السنة لعبد الله بن أحمد بن حنبل / بتحقيق محمد القحطاني ☐

كتب جامعة

شرح الطحاوية لابن أبي العز / بتحقيق التركي ☐

لوامع الأنوار للسفاريني / بتحقيق المكتب الإسلامي ☐

شرح النووية للهراس و ابن عيسى ☐

شرح العقيدة الواسطية للهراس ☐

الروضة الندية لابن فياض ☐

التحفة المهدية لابن مهدي / بتحقيق المحمود ☐

180

معارج القبول للحكمي / بتحقيق حلاق ☐

الإبانة الصغرى لابن بطة / بتحقيق رضا معطي ☐

أعلام السنة المنشورة للحكمي / بتحقيق خالد الردادي ☐

شرح السنة للبرهاري / بتحقيق محمد القحطاني ☐

متون عقدية

حاشية على ابن القاسم على الأصول الثلاثة ☐

مسائل الجاهلية لابن عبد الوهاب ☐

كشف الشبهات لابن عبد الوهاب / بتحقيق القحطاني ☐

فتح المجيد لعبد الرحمن آل الشيخ / بتحقيق الفريان ☐

حاشية على الدرة المضية لابن قاسم ☐

الحموية الكبرى لابن تيمية / بتحقيق التويجري ☐

الواسطية لابن تيمية / بتحقيق أشرف عبد المقصود ☐

الـمـلل والفرق

الملل و النحل للشهرستاني / بتحقيق أحمد فهمي ☐

مقالات الإسلاميين للأشعري / بتحقيق محمد محي الدين ☐

الفِصَل لابن حزم ☐

الفَرْق بين الفِرَق للبغدادي / بتحقيق محمد محي الدين ☐

عقائد الثلاث و السبعين فرقة / بتحقيق الغامدي ☐

الموسوعة الميسرة في الأديان و المذاهب المعاصرة للندوة العالمية ☐

III

تاريخ المذاهب الفقهية

الفكر السامي للحجوي / بتحقيق أيمن شعبان	
المدخل إلى دراسة المدارس و المذاهب المعاصرة	

كتب الخلاف

الأوسط لابن المنذر / بتحقيق صغير حنيف	
الإشراف على مذاهب العلماء / بتحقيق صغير حنيف	
حلية العلماء لقفال الشال / بتحقيق درادكه	
البحر الزخار لابن يحيى / بتحقيق القاضي عبد الله	
بداية المجتهد لابن رشد / بتحقيق حلاق	

كتب المذاهب الفقهية

المبسوط للسرخسي	
فتح القدير لابن الهمام	
الفتاوى الهندية	
المدونة لمالك	
شرح الزرقاني على مختصر خليل / عليه حاشية مهمة للبناني	
الأم للشافعي	
المجموع شرح المهذب للنووي / بتحقيق المطيعي	
الروضة للنووي	
المغني لابن قدامة / بتحقيق التركي	
الإنصاف للمرداوي / بتحقيق الفقي	
المحلى لابن حزم / بتحقيق البنداري	

لغة الفقه

طلِبّة الطَّلبة للنسفي

غريب ألفاظ المدونة للجبي / الطبعة المغربية

الزاهر في غريب ألفاظ الشافعي لأبي منصور الأزهري

المُطّلِع على أبواب المقنع للبعلي / طبع مع المبدع للبرهان ابن مفلح

التعريفات للجرجاني

الكليات للعكبري / بتحقيق الدرويش و آخر

أعلام الفقه وطبقاتهم

ترتيب المدارك للقاضي عياض

طبقات الشافعية للسبكي

طبقات الحنابلة لابن أبي يعلى

ذيل الطبقات لابن رجب / مع الطبقات لابن أبي يعلى

الفوائد البهية في طبقات الحنفية للكنوي

طبقات الفقهاء للشيرازي

كتب الأخلاق

الآداب الشرعية لابن مفلح / بتحقيق الأرناؤوط

غذاء الألباب للسفاريني

مختصر منهاج القاصدين للمقدسي / بتحقيق علي الحلبي

مدارج السالكين لابن القيم

أدب الدنيا للماوردي / بتحقيق السواس

جمع الوسائل في شرح الشمائل للقارئ / بهامشه حاشية للمناوي

III

تاريخ القواعد الفقهية

القواعد الفقهية ليعقوب الباحسين

كتب القواعد الفقهية

الفروق للقرافي

الأشباه و النظائر للسيوطي

الأشباه و النظائر لابن نجيم

القواعد لابن رجب / بتحقيق مشهور آل سلمان

درر الحكام شرح مجلة الإحكام لعلي حيدر / بتحقيق ترجمة فهمي

موسوعة القواعد الفقهية للبورنو

شرح منظومة القواعد الفقهية

إيضاح الدلائل لعبد الرحيم بن عبد الله / بتحقيق عمر السبيل

تاريخ أصول الفقه

أصول الفقه نشأته و تطوره لشعبان بن إسماعيل

الفكر الأصولي لعبد الوهاب أبو سليمان

كتب أصول الفقه المطبوعة

الدليل الجامع إلى كتب أصول الفقه المطبوعة لشامل شاهين

كتب أصول الفقه

الرسالة للشافعي / بتحقيق أحمد شاكر

البرهان لأبي المعالي / بتحقيق الديب

المستصفى للغزالي

184

المعتمد لأبي الحسين البصري	☐
المحصول للرازي / بتحقيق جابر العلواني	☐
الإحكام للآمدي	☐
كنز الوصول للبزدوي	☐
البدائع لابن الساعاتي	☐
البحر المحيط للزركشي / بتحقيق الأشقر	☐
روضة الناظر لابن قدامة / بتحقيق النملة	☐
شرح مختصر الروضة للطوفي / بتحقيق التركي	☐
مذكرة أصول الفقه للشنقيطي / بتحقيق سامي العربي	☐
الموافقات للشاطبي / بتحقيق مشهور آل سلمان	☐
شرح مختصر التحرير لابن النجار	☐
مقاصد الشريعة الإسلامية لابن عاشور	☐
إعلام الموقعين لابن القيم	☐

أهمية التاريخ

الإعلان بالتوبيخ لمن ذم التاريخ للسخاوي / بتحقيق فراز (مستشرق)	☐
منهج كتابة التاريخ لمحمد السلمي	☐

كتب التاريخ (تاريخ التاريخ)

علم التاريخ عند المسلمين لفرانز / ترجمة صالح العلي	☐
مصادر السيرة و تقويمها لفاروق حمادة	☐

III

تاريخ العرب قبل الإسلام

المفصل في تاريخ العرب لجواد علي

مكة في عصر ما قبل الإسلام لأبي الفضل

السيرة النبوية

السيرة لابن هشام / بتحقيق التدمري

الروض الأنف للسهيلي / بتحقيق طه سعيد

زاد المعاد لابن القيم / بتحقيق الأرناؤوطان

الفصول في سيرة الرسول لابن كثير / بتحقيق مستو و آخر

مختصر السيرة لمحمد بن عبد الوهاب / طبعة وزارة الشئون الإسلامية

السيرة النبوية لمهدي رزق الله

صحيح السيرة للطرهوني

السيرة الصحيحة لأكرم العمري

الخلافة الراشدة

عصر الخلافة لأكرم العمري

جولة في عصر الخلافة لمحمد السيد الوكيل

تاريخ ما بعد الخلافة الراشدة

تاريخ ابن جرير

البداية و النهاية لابن كثير / بتحقيق التركي

الكامل لابن الأثير

الدولة العثمانية لياغي

عنوان المجد في تاريخ نجد لابن بشر ☐

تاريخ عسير هاشم النعمي ☐

تحفة المستفيد بتاريخ الأحساء في القديم و الجديد ☐

مملكة الحجاز لوهيم طالب ☐

التعليم في مكة و المدينة آخر العهد العثماني لمحمد ☐

شبه الجزيرة في عهد الملك عبد العزيز للزركلي ☐

السعوديون و الحل الإسلامي لجلال كشك ☐

تاريخ المملكة العربية السعودية لعبد الله صالح العثيمين ☐

تاريخ أوروبا

أوروبا العصور الوسطى لسعيد عبد الفتاح ☐

التاريخ الأوروبي الحديث للبطريق و آخر ☐

التراجم

الإصابة لابن حجر ☐

سير أعلام النبلاء للذهبي / بتحقيق الأرناؤوط ☐

تذكرة الحفاظ للذهبي / بتحقيق المعلمي ☐

إنباء الغمر لابن حجر ☐

تهذيب التهذيب لابن حجر ☐

تقريب التهذيب لابن حجر / بتحقيق الباكستاني ☐

الضوء اللامع للسخاوي ☐

البدر الطالع للشوكاني / بتحقيق العمري ☐

III

شذرات الذهب لابن العماد / بتحقيق الأرناؤوط □

الأعلام الزركلي / هناك تتمة ما قام به محمد خير رمضان □

معجم المصنفين لكحالة / هناك تتمة ما قام به محمد خير رمضان □

المعجمات اللغوية

تهذيب اللغة للأزهري □

الصحاح للجوهري / بتحقيق العطار □

مقاييس اللغة لابن فارس / بتحقيق عبد السلام هارون □

القاموس للفيروزآبادي □

لسان العرب لابن منظور / الطبعة الملونة □

المصباح للفيومي / بتحقيق محمد الصادق □

شرح القاموس للزبيدي □

أخطاء لغوية

تصحيح التصحيف للصفدي / بتحقيق الشرقاوي □

أخطاء لغوية شائعة للعدناني □

الحكم و الأمثال

مجمع الحكم و الأمثال للميداني / بتحقيق عبد السلام هارون □

الشعر العربي

الشعر و الشعراء لابن قتيبة / بتحقيق أحمد شاكر □

مختارات البارودي □

مجمع الحكم و الأمثال في الشعر العربي لقبّش □

علم الصرف

الممتع في التصريف لابن عصفور / بتحقيق فخر الدين قباوه

شرح مختصر العِزّي للتفتازاني / بتحقيق عبد العال مكرم

دروس في التصريف لمحمد محي الدين عبد الحميد

علم البلاغة

تاريخ البلاغة لشوقي ضيف

شرح التلخيص للبرقوني

الواضح في البلاغة لعوني

علم النحو

نشأة النحو لطنطاوي / بتحقيق الشناوي و آخر

شرح ملحة الإعراب لحريري

شرح الآجرومية لمحمد محي الدين عبد الحميد

شرح قطر الندى لابن هشام / بتحقيق محمد محي الدين

شرح ابن عقيل على الألفية / بتحقيق محمد محي الدين

أوضح المسالك لابن هشام / بتحقيق محمد محي الدين

همع الهوامع للسيوطي / بتحقيق عبد العال مكرم

مغني اللبيب لابن هشام / بتحقيق محمد محي الدين

أصول النحو للسيوطي / بتحقيق فجال

علم الإنشاء

معالم الكتابة لابن شيت / بتحقيق محمد شمس الدين

أدب الكاتب لابن قتيبة / بتحقيق محمد محي الدين

علم الإملاء (رسم القلم)

قواعد الإملاء لعبد السلام هارون

رسم القلم لأحمد الهاشمي

الثقافة الأدبية العربية

الكامل للمُبَرِّد / بتحقيق محمد الدالي

العقد الفريد لابن عبد ربه

تاريخ الأدب لشوقي ضيف

أصول النسب

اللباب في معرفة الأنساب للأشعري

القصد و الأمم لابن عبد البر

أنساب العرب

جمهرة أنساب العرب لابن حزم / بتحقيق عبد السلام هارون

فضل العرب

القرب في محبة العرب لزين الدين العراقي (الكردي) / طبعة مصرية

طبقات النساب و كتبهم

طبقات النسابين لبكر أبو زيد

ضبط الأسماء والأنساب

لُب اللباب للسيوطي / بتحقيق ابنا أحمد عبد العزيز

المغني لمحمد طاهر الهندي

تاريخ علم المنطق وحكمه

الرد على المنطقيين لابن تيمية / طبعة ترجمان السنة

صون المنطق والكلام عن فن المنطق والكلام / بتحقيق علي النشار

مفردات علم المنطق

المطلع على ايساغوجي الأنصاري

إيضاح المبهم من معاني السُّلَم للدمنهوري

آداب البحث والمناظرة لمحمد الأمين الشنقيطي

ضوابط المعرفة للميداني

كتب متفرقة

معجم البلدان لياقوت الحموي / بتحقيق فريد الجند

كشف الظنون لحاجي خليفة

الدرر السنية لابن القاسم

مجموعة الرسائل النجدية / طبعة دار العاصمة

فتاوى هيئة كبار العلماء للدويش / لم تكمل

جميع كتب شيخ الإسلام ابن تيمية وفتاويه

جميع كتب ابن القيم

جميع كتب ابن رجب

III

191

Glossary of Arabic Terms

'Aam [عَام]
Term used in Usool al-Fiqh denoting a general word.

Aayah, pl. Aayaat [آية جـ آيات]
Sign, miracle, verse from the Noble Qur.aan.

Adhaan [أَذَان]
The call to prayer, pronounced vocally to indicate the time of prayer has entered.

Ahl adh-Dhikr [أَهْلُ الذِّكْر]
Literally means, "People of Reminder", as occurs in the Qur.aan in Soorah al-Anbiyaa, Aayah 7:
> ***So ask the people of the Reminder [Scriptures –
> the Torah, the Gospel] if you do not know.***

Ahlul-Kalaam [أَهْلُ الْكَلام]
People of dialectical theology.

'Alayhim as-Salaam [عَلَيْه السَّلام]

Literally means, "Salutations be upon him." This is to be said every time reference is made to any of the Messengers and Prophets of Allaah.

Al-'Asr [الْعَصْر]

Literally means, "The Time"; It is also the name of the 103rd Soorah of the Qur.aan.

al-Hamdu Lillaah [الْحَمْدُ لله]

Literally means, "All Praise is due to Allaah."

Allaahu Akbar [الله أَكْبَر]

Literally means, "Allaah is the Greatest."

Allaahul-Musta'aan [الله الْمُسْتَعَان]

Literally means, "Allaah is the One from Whom Assistance is sought."

'Aqeedah, pl. 'Aqaa.id [عَقِيْدَة جـ عَقَائد]

Creed, belief, doctrine.

Athar, pl. Aathaar [أَثَر جـ آثَار]

A tradition, hadeeth, sunnah of the Messenger of Allaah.

Balaaghah [بَلاغَة]

Eloquence, good style, expressiveness, fluency.

Birr [برّ]

Righteousness, righteous deed, piety, charity, dutifulness, devotion, obedience, kindness, upright.

Daa'ee, pl. Du'aat [دَاعِي جــ دُعَاة]

One who engages in missionary work to invite all people to worship Allaah as One, without associating any partners with Him; in short - Islaam.

Da'eef [ضَعِيْف]

A weak hadeeth, narration.

Da'wah, pl. Da'waat [دَعْوَة جــ دَعْوَات]

Missionary work to invite all people to worship Allaah as One, without associating any partners with Him; in short - Islaam.

Deenaar, pl. Danaaneer [دِيْنَار جــ دَنَانِيْر]

A gold coin from the old Roman era weighing 4.233 gramms, equivalent to twenty dirhams during the time of the Messenger of Allaah (sal-Allaahu 'alayhi wa sallam).

Dirham, pl. Daraahim [دِرْهَم جــ دَرَاهِم]

A silver coin weighing 2.9 gramms, equivalent to a twenteith part of a deenaar during the time of the Messenger of Allaah (sal-Allaahu 'alayhi wa sallam).

Eemaan [إِيْمَان]

A firm belief in Allaah, the Angels, the Revealed Books, the Messengers. The Last Day and al-Qadar. It manifests itself in the heart, the tongue, and upon the limbs – and it increases with obedience to Allaah and decreases with disobedience to Him.

Faahishah, pl. Fawaahish [فَاحِشَة جــ فَوَاحِش]

Obscenity (such as adultery, lesbianism, sodomy, incest). shameful deed, obscene act, filthy act, abominalbe act.

Fajr [فَجْر]
Pre-dawn prayer; the first obligatory prayer of the day.

Fareedah, pl. Faraa.id [فَرِيْضَة جـ فَرَائض]
Prescribed shares of inheritance; Law of inheritance.

Fard 'Ayn [فَرْضُ عَيْن]
Personal obligation, individual duty.

Fard Kifaayah [فَرْض كفَاية]
Collective obligation.

Fatwa, pl. Fataawa [فَتْوَى جـ فَتَاوَى]
Legal ruling based upon the Qur.aan and the Sunnah, passed by a Scholar in response to a question.

Faqeeh, pl. Fuqahaa [فَقِيْه جـ فُقَهَاء]
Jurist, jurisprudent, legal expert; one who is distinguished in his knowledge and understanding of fiqh.

Fiqh [فقْه]
Islaamic jurisprudence.

Furqaan [فُرْقَان]
Discriminator, separator between right and wrong, criterion. Another name for the Qur.aan.

Ghusl [غُسْل]
Major ritual ablution, washing oneself, bathing.

Haafiz, pl. Huffaaz [حُفَّاظ ــجـ حَافظ]

One whose knowledge of hadeeth is more than that which he knows not; His comprehensive knowledge of hadeeth places him at a recognised level above the Muhaddith.

Hadeeth, pl. Ahaadeeth [أَحَادِيْث ــجـ حَدِيْث]

Literally means, "sayings" and could refer to the recorded quotes of anyone. Usually, it is the title given to the collection of recorded words, actions and tacit approvals of the Prophet Muhammad (sal-Allaahu 'alayhi wa sallam), which serve as an explanation of the meaning of the Noble Qur.aan.

Hajj [حَجّ]

The "major pilgrimage". The once in a lifetime obligation (only if one possesses the means) of pilgrimage to Makkah; made up of specified rites performed between the 8th to the 13th day of Dhul-Hijjah (the twelfth month of the Islaamic Hijrah year). It is one of the five pillars of Islaam.

Hakeem, pl. Hukamaa [حُكَمَاء ــجـ حَكِيْم]

Wise man, wise, sagacious, prudent, judicious, reasonable, sensible, shrewd.

Halaal [حَلال]

Lawful, legal, licit, allowed, allowable, permissible, permitted.

Hanafee, pl. Hanafiyyah / Ahnaaf [أَحْنَاف / حَنَفِيَّة ــجـ حَنَفِيّ]

An adherent to, or a student of the School of Islaamic Jurisprudence which is based upon the teachings of Abu Haneefah Nu'maan ibn Thaabit ibn Zootaa ibn Marzubaan (died in Baghdad 148 Hijree / 767 AD).

Hanbalee, pl. Hanaabilah [حَنْبَلِي جـ ـ حَنَابِلة]

An adherent to, or a student of the School of Islaamic Juris-prudence which is based upon the teachings of Abu 'Abdullaah Ahmad ibn Muhammad ibn Hanbal ash-Shaybaanee (died in Baghdad 241 Hijree / 855 AD).

Haraam [حَرَام]

Unlawful, illegal, illicit, illegitimate, forbidden, prohibited, banned, taboo, disallowed, barred.

Hasan [حَسَن]

Literally means, good and handsome. Ibn Hajar explains it to be that hadeeth which fulfills the conditions of the "saheeh" ex-cept that the precision of one or more of its narrators is of a lesser standard.

Hijrah, pl. Hijraat [هِجْرَة جـ ـ هِجْرَات]

Emigration, expatriation, exodus, immigration (to), migra-tion.

Hikmah, pl. Hikam [حِكْمَة]

Wisdom, sapience, sageness, sagacity, judiciousness, prudence, foresight, insight, reason, reasonableness.

Hizbiyyah [حِزْبِيَّة]

Partisanship, factionalism, party life (spirit, activities), partial-ity, bias.

'Ibaadah [عِبَادَة]

Act of worship, religious observances, forms of worship, devo-tions.

Ihkaam [إِحْكَام]

Accuracy, precision, exactness, correctness, perfection, exactitude, definitude.

Ijtihaad, pl. Ijtihaadaat [إِجْتِهَادَات ـجـ إِجْتِهَاد]

The effort a jurist makes in order to deduce the law, which is not self-evident, from it sources.

Imaam, pl. A.immah [أَئِمَّة ـجـ إِمَام]

A distinguished and recognised scholar; Generally recognised to be at a level above the 'Allaamah, and often referred to as a Mujaddid (reformer and reviver of the religion). Also used to refer to the one who leads the prayer.

I'raab [إِعْرَاب]

Arabic grammar term denoting the analysis of a word in a sentence and, where applicable, any change affected upon it by a preceding word resulting in a modification/change reaching the end of the word.

'Ishaa [عشَاء]

Night prayer; the last obligatory prayer of the day.

Islaam [إِسْلام]

Submission, surrender, obedience to the Will of Allaah.

Ism, pl. Asmaa. [أَسْمَاء ـجـ إِسْم]

Popularly referred to as name, divine name of Allaah.

Isnaad, pl. Asaaneed [أَسَانِيْد ـجـ إِسْنَاد]

Chain of narration.

198

Israa.eel [إِسْرَائِيْل]

Israelites, the ancient Jews.

Janaabah [جَنَابَة]

Major ritual impurity, grave impurity, ceremonial impurity, the greater incident.

Jannah, pl. Jannaat [جَنَّة جـ جَنَّات]

Heaven, paradise, garden.

Jihaad [جهَاد]

To strive hard, or to fight to defend one's life, property, freedom, and religion. It can also refer to an attempt to free other people from oppression and tyranny. Importantly, Islaam strongly opposes the kidnapping, terrorising, or hijacking of civilians, even during war.

Jumu'ah [جُمُعَة]

The Friday prayer performed in jamaa'ah after the khutbah. This is in place of the Salaat az-Zhuhr.

**Kaafir, pl. Ḳaafiroon / Kuffaar / Kafarah
[كافِر جـ كافِرُوْن / كُفَّار / كَفَرَة]**

Disbeliever, infidel, non-believer, one who disbelieves, unbelieveing person, one who rejects (faith), one who denies.

Kalaam [كَلام]

Speech, rhetoric, talk, words, speaking, address, saying, lecture.

Khutbah, pl. Khutab [خُطْبَة جـ خُطَب]

A public sermon, address, speech.

Laa ilaaha il-Allaah [لاَ إِلَهَ إِلَّا الله]

Literally means, "There is none truly worthy of worship except Allaah."

Laa-Ilaaha illaa Huwa [لا إِلَهَ إِلَّ هُوَ]

Literally means, "There is none truly worthy of worship except Him."

Maalikee, pl. Maalikiyyah [مَالكيّ جـ مَالكيّة]

An adherent to, or a student of the School of Islaamic Jurisprudence which is based upon the teachings of Abu 'Abdullaah Maalik ibn Anas ibn Maalik ibn 'Amr al-Asbahi (died in Madeenah 179 Hijree / 795 AD).

Madhhab, pl. Madhaahib [مَذْهَب جـ مّذَاهِب]

School, school of Islaamic jurisprudence, school of religious law, doctrine, persuasion, sect, way, manner.

Manhaj, pl. Manaahij [مَنْهَج جـ مَنَاهِج]

Methodology, manner, approach, procedure.

Mansookh [مَنْسُوْخ]

Abrogated, repealed legal rule.

Masjid, pl. Masaajid [مَسْجِد جـ مَسَاجِد]

The Muslim's place of worship.

Matn, pl. Mutoon [مَتْن جـ مُتُوْن]

Text, wording, letter, quotation, subject matter.

Mubtadi', pl. Mubtadi'ah [مُبْتَدِع جــ مُبْتَدَعَة]
Innovator, heretic, heterodox, heresiarch, dissenter.

Muhaddith, pl. Muhaddithoon [مُحَدِّث جــ مُحَدِّثُوْن]
A distinguished scholar of hadeeth. His level of knowledge is lesser than that of the Haafiz.

Mujaahid, pl. Mujaahidoon [مُجَاهِد جــ مُجَاهِدُوْن]
Struggler; one engaged in jihaad.

Mujtahid, pl. Mujtahidoon [مُجْتَهِد جــ مُجْتَهِدُوْن]
Qualified scholar, diligent jurist, diligent interpreter of Sharee'ah law, independent reasoner, judicious reasoner.

Mukhassis [مُخَصِّص]
Usool al-Fiqh term denoting specifying proof.

Munaafiq, pl. Munaafiqoon [مُنَافِق جــ مُنَافِقُوْن]
Hypocrite. One who makes apparent that which is contrary to what is in his heart. The signs of a hypocrite are four:
i) when he is entrusted, he breaks the trust;
ii) when he speaks, he lies;
iii) when he promises, he breaks his promise;
iv) when he argues, he behaves immorally.

Muqayyad [مُقَيَّد]
Usool al-Fiqh term denoting a confined and qualified word.

Musannaf [مُصَنَّف]

A comprehensive collection of ahaadeeth in which the traditions are assembled and arranged in various "books" or "chapters", each dealing with a particular topic. To this class belong the Muwatta of Imaam Maalik, the Saheeh of Muslim, and similar works.

Mushrik, pl. Mushrikoon [مُشْرِك جــ مُشْرِكُوْن]

Polytheist. One who associates partners in worship with Allaah.

Musnad [مُسْنَد]

A collection of traditions listing the names of the Companions in alphabetical order. The most important and exhaustive of all the musnad works available is that of Imaam Ahmad ibn Hanbal.

Mustadrak [مُسْتَدْرَك]

A collection of traditions which the compiler, having accepted the conditions laid down by a previous compiler, collects together such other traditions as fulfil those conditions and were missed by his perdecessor. To this class belongs the Mustadrak of al-Haakim an-Neesaabooree, who assembled a large number of ahaadeeth which fulfilled the stringent conditions laid down by al-Bukhaaree and Muslim, but were not included in their Saheeh compilations.

Mustalah al-Hadeeth [مُصْطَلَح الْحَدِيْث]

Science of hadeeth and it's terminology.

Mutashaddiq, pl. Mutashaddiqoon [مُتَشَدِّق جــ مُتَشَدِّقُوْن]

Ranter and raver.

Mutlaq [مُطْلَق]

Usool al-Fiqh term denoting an unconfined and unrestricted word.

Muttaqee, pl. Muttaqoon [مُتَّقُوْن ـﺟ مُتَّقِيّ]

One who fears Allaah. The pious, the righteous, one who shields oneself against the wrath of Allaah, one who wards off Allaah's wrath by devoting himself to worship and good deeds.

Nahoo [نَحُو]

Arabic grammar, syntax.

Nass, pl. Nusoos [نُصُوْص ـﺟ نَصّ]

Plain and clear text. Popularly referred to as the texts of the Qur. aan and the Hadeeth.

Nughayr [نُغَيْر]

Little birdy, little bulbul.

Qadr, pl. Aqdaar [أَقْدَار ـﺟ قَدَر]

Predetermined decree of Allaah.

Qiyaam [قِيَام]

Standing. Standing posture assumed during the salaah. Being on one's legs.

Qu'ood [قُعُوْد]

Sitting. Sitting posture assumed during the salaah. Sitting knelt down on one's legs.

Qur.aan [قُرْآن]

Compiled divine revelations from Allaah to Prophet Muhammad; The Holy Book of the Muslims.

Radhi-yAllaahu 'anhu / 'anhaa / 'anhumaa / 'anhum
[رَضِيَ الله عَنْهُ / عَنْهَا / عَنْهُمَا / عَنْهُمْ]

Literally means, "May Allaah be pleased with him / her / with the two of them / with them."

Rahima-hullaah / hallaah / humullaah
[رَحِمَهُ / رَحِمَهَا / رَحِمَهُمُ الله]

Literally means, "May Allaah have mercy upon him / her / upon them."

Rajul, pl. Rijaal [رَجُل جـ رِجَال]

Literally means men; Technically it refers to the male narrators of ahaadeeth.

Ramadhaan [رَمَضَان]

Ninth month of the Islaamic Hijrah year. Fasting has been prescribed from dawn til dusk for the duration of this month.

Riqaaq, pl. Raqaa.iq [رِقَاق جـ رَقَائِق]

Heart-warming narrations. Narrations that evoke warmth and tenderness in the heart.

Rukoo' [رُكُوْع]

Bowing down. Bending at the waist, stooping. Bowing posture assumed during the salaah.

Rusookh [رُسُوْخ]

Steadfastness, firmly established. Well-grounded, unshakeable, immovable, fixed, rooted.

Sahaabee / Saahib, pl. Sahaabah / As.haab
[صَحَابِي / صَاحِب جــ صَحَابَة / أَصْحَاب]

The close companions of the Prophet Muhammad (sal-Allaahu 'alayhi wa sallam).

Saheeh, pl. Sihaah [صَحِيْح جــ صِحَاح]

Authentic, correct.

Sal-Allaahu 'alayhi wa sallam [صَلَّى الله عَلَيْه وَ سَلَّم]

Literally means, "May Allaah send prayers and salutations upon him." This is to be said every time reference is made to the final Messenger of Allaah, Muhammad.

Salaah, pl. Salawaat [صَلاَة جــ صَلَوَات]

Term referred to specific supplications and actions, correctly understood as prayers. The Muslims are required to perform five daily prayers. It is one of the five pillars of Islaam.

Salaf, pl. Aslaaf [سَلَف جــ أَسْلاَف]

The first three generations of Muslims. Popularly referred to as "as-Salaf as-Saalih" [السَّلَفُ الصَّلِح] - the pious predecessors.

Sami'a Allaahu li-man Hamidah [سَمِعَ الله لِمَنْ حَمِدَه]

Literally means, "Allaah listens to the one who praises Him".

Sarf [صَرْف]

Morphology (linguistics) - the study of the structure and content of word forms.

Shaafi'ee, pl. Shaafi'iyyah [شَافِعِيَّة ـجـ شَافِعِيّ]

An adherent to, or a student of the School of Islaamic Juris-prudence which is based upon the teachings of Abu 'Abdullaah Muhammad ibn Idrees ash-Shaafi'ee (died in Fustat, Egypt 204 Hijree / 820 AD).

Sha'baan [شَعْبَان]

Eighth month of the Islaamic Hijrah year.

Sharee'ah, pl. Sharaa.i' [شَرَائِع ـجـ شَرِيْعَة]

The Islaamic Law, in particular, what is stated in the texts of the Qur.aan and the Sunnah.

Shaykh, pl. Shuyookh, Mashaa.ikh, Mashaayikh
[مَشَايِخ / مَشَائِخ / شُيُوْخ ـجـ شَيْخ]

Correctly referred to as a religious scholar; however, it is also referred to one who is elderly.

Shaytaan, pl. Shayaateen [شَيَاطِيْن ـجـ شَيْطَان]

Satan. The evil one, evil spirit, devil, demon.

Sifah, pl. Sifaat [صِفَات ـجـ صِفَة]

Description, attribute, characteristic, quality, trait.

Subhaanahu wa Ta'aala [سُبْحَانَهُ وَ تَعَالَى]

Literally means, "How perfect He is, the Almighty"; Complete meaning: "I exalt Him and elevate Him above having any defects or deficiencies.".

Sujood / Sajdah, pl. Sajadaat [سُجُوْد / سَجْدَة جـ سَجَدَات]

The prostration posture in salaah.

Sunnah, pl. Sunan [سُنَّة جـ سُنَن]

Way, mode, manner; correctly referred to as the words, actions and tacit approvals of the Prophet Muhammad (sal-Allaahu 'alayhi wa sallam), which serve as an explanation of the meaning of the Noble Qur.aan.

Tafseer, pl. Tafaaseer [تَفْسِيْر جـ تَفَاسِيْر]

Commentary, exegesis, explanation.

Tahajjud [تَهَجُّد]

Supererogatory night prayer - best performed during the last third of the night.

Taqwa [تَقْوَى]

Fear, dread, awe. Piety to Allaah, fear of Allaah, warding off Allaah's wrath, being conscious of Allaah, devotion, devoutness.

Ta.seel [تَأْصِيْل]

Firmly established, deep seated, taking root, striking root, becoming deep-rooted.

Tathabbut [تَثَبُّت]

Verification, checking, making sure, certitude, conviction, ascertainment, certainty.

Tawheed [تَوْحِيْد]

Singling out. To single out Allaah ('Azza wa Jall) alone for worship.

Tayyibaat [طَيِّبَات]

Pure women, good women.

Thabaat [ثَبَات]

Firmness, fortitude, perseverance, tenacity.

Tharthaar, pl. Tharthaaroon [ثَرْثَار جـ ثَرْثَارُوْن]

Talkative, chatty, gossipy, garrulous, loquacious, chatterbox.

Ummah, pl. Umam [أُمَّة جـ أُمَم]

Community of Muslims, the Muslim nation.

'Umrah [عُمْرَة]

The "minor pilgrimage." It has fewer rites than the "major pilgrimage" (Hajj). In general, it may be performed at any time of the year.

Usool ad-Deen [أُصُوْل الدِّين]

Principles of the religion.

Usool al-Fiqh [أُصُوْل الْفِقْه]

Principles of Islaamic Jurisprudence.

Wahee [وَحي]

Revelation, divine guidance, inspiration, afflatus.

Waajib [وَاجب]

Obligatory, mandatory, compulsory.

Wudoo [وُضُوْء]

Ablution, minor ritual ablution, washing oneself in a prescribed manner in preparation for salaah or other acts of worship.

Zakaah, pl. Zakawaat [زَكَاة جـ زَكَوَات]

The alms tax deducted from the Muslims wealth at a rate of 2.5%, and distributed to the poor and needy. It is one of the five pillars of Islaam.

Notes